PUSEY

The U. S. A. astride the globe.

DATE DUE			

THE U.S.A.
ASTRIDE
THE GLOBE

BY MERLO J. PUSEY

The Supreme Court Crisis

Big Government: Can We Control It?

Charles Evans Hughes
(two volumes)

Eisenhower The President

The Way We Go to War

The U.S.A. Astride the Globe

THE
U.S.A.
ASTRIDE
THE
GLOBE

722968

Merlo J. Pusey

HOUGHTON MIFFLIN COMPANY BOSTON

1971

First Printing c

International Standard Book Number: 0-395-12717-3
Library of Congress Catalog Card Number: 74-158150
Printed in the United States of America

Preface

THIS BOOK is a sequel to *The Way We Go to War,* published in 1969. In that volume I dealt with the President's usurpation of the war power, which the Constitution assigned to Congress. Presidential wars have assumed especially serious proportions because the United States maintains the most formidable military establishment of all time. In other words, unprecedented power is at the almost exclusive disposal of the President. It seems pertinent, therefore, to review the extent of this power and how it has been used.

The purpose behind this volume is not to attack the military. Nor is it to aid or support the neoisolationism that is finding expression in some American circles. Rather, the book is an attempt to look candidly at our excessively military posture in the world, for which Congress and both our major political parties are responsible no less than the President. As a nation we have allowed ourselves the dubious luxury of throwing our military weight around regardless of whether our vital interests have been involved. Holding firmly to the belief that war and the steps that lead to it are too important to be left solely to the military, I make no apology for expressing a layman's viewpoint on this matter.

The book could not have been written without the inves-

tigations conducted by the Senate Subcommittee on United
States Security Agreements and Commitments Abroad headed
by Senator Stuart Symington. I have relied heavily on the
findings of this subcommittee and its staff, which published,
in heavily censored volumes, at least part of the testimony
taken in closed sessions during 1969 and 1970. The general
picture these hearings present is one of overextended military commitments and reckless use of power. The conclusions drawn by the subcommittee are in harmony with views
independently expressed by many other observers of the
world scene. My effort has been to present, from these many
sources, a concise account of what our military has been doing abroad and to assess some of the consequences of our
excessive preoccupation with military force in the name of
peace and freedom.

Many officials, colleagues, and friends have contributed to
the thoughts expressed here, and others have tempered the
conclusions by their criticism. For all this help I am grateful.
My thanks go also to my wife and to the editors of Houghton
Mifflin Company for helpful suggestions and to Mrs. John G.
De Gooyer for typing the manuscript.

Contents

Contents

I

The Eagle's-Eye View

CAN THE UNITED STATES pull back from its almost worldwide police role? Since World War II this country has functioned as a sort of global guardian against Communism, with few limitations on its assumed responsibilities. American military forces have been stationed all the way from our front yard of defense, the Western Hemisphere, and our cultural birthplace, Western Europe, to the remote corners of Asia. Two major "police actions" have taken more than 75,000 American lives. We have built and continue to maintain a formidable array of military bases in nearly every section of the globe. At the same time we manage to give the impression that we intend to intervene in local conflicts whenever Communism appears to be an issue.

The tendency in Washington has been to renounce the role of global policemen but to go ahead with the policing. Although the methods, the rationale, and the intensity of military operations have varied from one administration to another, the general posture of American dominance and the casual use of military power to make our wishes prevail have been very persistent in the postwar era. In the space of only two generations the United States has emerged from the position of an isolated and almost unarmed bystander on the world scene to that of a superpower which sits astride the globe and attempts to decide the shape of the future.

At least in some measure the superpower role was thrust upon us. President Kennedy spoke of the United States being "by destiny rather than choice, the watchman on the walls of world freedom." [1] In the ferment and chaos of the late forties and fifties, the United States was almost the sole center of order and power in the free world. If any nation or group of nations was to stand up against the onslaught of the Communist revolution, it had to draw strength in some measure from Washington. President Nixon took note of the forces which pushed us into the superpower role in his 1970 State of the Union address:

> . . . because of America's overwhelming military and economic strength, the weakness of other major free world powers and the inability of scores of newly independent nations to defend — let alone govern — themselves, America had to assume the major burden for the defense of freedom in the world.[2]

But the prostration resulting from World War II was a temporary state of affairs. Japan and the industrial nations of Europe soon regained their economic strength and a substantial measure of political stability. Many new countries emerged from the wreckage of the colonial empires and gave new dimensions to the struggle for dignity, equality, and prosperity in the world. It was inevitable, with the mere passing of time, that the American stance as a sort of free-world Hercules would be challenged and that the American presence in remote corners of the earth should become more troublesome. Yet we have moved from one venture to an-

[1] Quoted by Ronald Steel in *Pax Americana* (New York: Viking, 1967), p. 12.
[2] *Washington Post*, January 23, 1970, p. A14.

other without ever formulating a comprehensive policy on the use of our national power. In recent years the country has heard much of a change in "profile" and curtailment of military spending, coupled with a somewhat uncertain retreat from Vietnam, but the image of a colossus casting a long shadow has not basically changed.

Some observers see this effort to play the role of global protector as naked imperialism. Professor Noam Chomsky, apparently drawing more on venom than on his powers of observation, has been telling us for years that the United States has become "the most aggressive nation in the world" and that "the present world problem is not 'containing China' but containing the United States." [3] Vietnam drove even General David M. Shoup, a seasoned product of our military establishment who was commandant of the Marine Corps before his retirement in 1963, to complain that "militarism in America is in full bloom and promises a future of vigorous self-pollination." [4] Sage and conservative George D. Aiken, Republican senator from Vermont, expressed the belief that "the Defense Department has been running hog wild. Some people have got worried for fear we've become a military government." [5] Compared to many other comments that were floating in the atmosphere during the late sixties and the early seventies, these gibes were relatively mild. The country which has sincerely tried to export the luxuries of democracy and peace is reaping a harvest of brickbats from the center as well as the Left and Right. Even when ample allowance is made for disgruntled fanatics mouthing the patent distortions of Peking and Hanoi, enough ugly truth remains to make millions of sensitive Americans wince.

It is not necessary to blacken the motives of any President

[3] *American Power and the New Mandarins* (New York: Pantheon, 1969), p. 385, 378.
[4] *The Atlantic*, April, 1969, p. 56.
[5] Quoted by Warren Unna in the *Washington Post*, March 23, 1969, pp. 1–2.

to see the damage that has been done to our moral standing in the world. Let us assume for the sake of seeing our present predicament more clearly that the rhetoric of peace and self-determination that pours out of Washington in great volume at frequent intervals is entirely sincere — that the overextension of our military power is solely a result of bad judgment, excessive risk-taking, or miscalculation of our own vital interests. Regardless of what gloss we may put upon it, the record of how we have used our power since World War II does not inspire much confidence in our friends in other countries, and when it is coupled with an excessive American military presence in many parts of the world the danger of mounting antagonism becomes obvious.

One measure of our preoccupation with military might may be seen in our leadership of the nuclear parade. Since the Soviet Union became a nuclear power it has been obvious that the United States would have to develop and maintain enough nuclear capacity to discourage Moscow from trying to wipe us out with a single first strike. How much nuclear power would this require? No one could be certain, of course, but Robert S. McNamara once suggested while he was still secretary of defense that the USSR might think the loss of one fifth to one fourth of its population and destruction of one half of its industry too big a price to pay for a first-strike "victory." That price could be exacted of the Soviet Union, McNamara went on to say, by dropping 400 warheads of one megaton each on the right targets. At the time, however, the United States is said to have had more than 4200 deliverable nuclear warheads, nearly four times as many as the Soviet Union then possessed and more than ten times the number needed to discourage a surprise attack according to the McNamara formula.

We are also indebted to McNamara for another candid acknowledgment of our enormous contributions to the nuclear arms race. In 1961 the Kennedy administration, in which he was a key figure, concluded that Russia was capable of building a powerful force of intercontinental ballistic missiles that might be able to wipe out the American carrier fleet. "We had no evidence," the Secretary of Defense later confessed, "that the Soviets did plan, in fact, fully to use that capacity." [6] On the basis of what proved to be unfounded fear, the United States rushed ahead with a crash missile program, while in fact the USSR proceeded much more moderately. The Institute for Strategic Studies reports that Russia was ahead of the United States, with 35 ICBMs to our 18 in 1960, although the United States then had 32 surface-launched ballistic missiles (SLBM) compared to none for the Soviet Union. During the next five years American ICBMs proliferated to 934, while the Soviet Union acquired only 224. In the same year (1965) we had 464 submarine-launched ballistic missiles; the USSR had 107.[7] Apparently it was then Moscow's turn to be frightened. From 1965 to 1970 the Russians built furiously, with the result of surpassing the American inventory of 1054 ICBMs. President Nixon estimated Soviet ICBMs at 1290 and Soviet submarine-launched ballistic missiles at 300 (compared to 656 for the U.S.) at the end of 1970. "Clearly," McNamara admitted, after the damage had been done, "the Soviet build-up is in part a reaction to our own build-up since the beginning of this decade." [8]

It is not the purpose of this volume to compare the military establishments of the two superpowers. Both have con-

---

[6] Robert S. McNamara, *The Essence of Security,* a compilation of his policy statements as Secretary of Defense, 1961–1968 (New York: Harper & Row, 1968), pp. 57–58.
[7] "United States Foreign Policy for the 1970's; a New Strategy for Peace," report by President Nixon to Congress, February 18, 1970, p. 91.
[8] Quoted by Helen B. Shaffer in "Nuclear Balance of Terror: 25 Years After Alamogordo," *Editorial Research Reports,* 1970, Vol. II, No. 1, July 1, 1970.

tributed much to the incalculable hazards of mass incineration that now bedevil mankind. Fairness compels us to recognize, however, that the United States has led the parade. With 95 per cent of the nuclear power of the non-Communist world, our policy-makers apparently assumed that safety could be found in being far ahead in the race. That proved to be a colossal illusion. The Johnson administration finally came to realize that nothing we could do would prevent the Soviet Union from developing a strategic posture comparable to our own and that neither power would find security in adding further overkill capacity. This focused interest on negotiations in place of further proliferation, but it is not surprising that Moscow, having previously been badly outdistanced in the race, was skeptical of our intentions and took a long time to come to the conference table.

Despite the missile rattling of his 1968 campaign, President Nixon, when confronted by the responsibilities of office, concluded that either sharp cutbacks or sharp increases in our strategic nuclear power might have disastrous results. That conclusion led to the strategic arms limitation talks (SALT) in Vienna and Helsinki. Hope for agreement seemed to rest chiefly on the fact that the two superpowers had reached a large measure of parity in their nuclear arsenals which might make feasible a freeze at existing levels. If that is the only principle on which arms limitation is likely to succeed, and it was the basis of the only major arms control treaty ever negotiated — the naval agreement at Washington in 1922, what a pity it is that serious negotiations came at the 1000-ICBM level instead of the 100-ICBM level or some other level less fraught with peril for all mankind! The other observation that springs irresistibly out of this experience is that a less dominating American posture in other areas might also relieve tensions and foster agreements.

It is difficult to know, of course, what an adequate defense

is. Senator Stuart Symington has noted that "more changes
have occurred in the concept of an adequate defense posture
during the last 25 years than in the previous history of mankind." [9] But only the United States has had an $80 billion
defense budget in recent years, compared to an estimated
$42,140,000,000 budget for the USSR. Only the United
States has spotted the globe with military bases. Security has
been piled upon security without much regard for the effects
upon domestic programs or upon other countries that are
not able to keep up with such a furious pace in the military
field. The least that can be said is that one has to look at
the network of American bases against the background of a
three-pronged nuclear defense system. It consists of (1)
enough intercontinental ballistic missiles to destroy any
enemy many times over, (2) a formidable fleet of submarines
ready to fire their devastating Polaris missiles from beneath
the seas, many of which will be more formidable when supplied with Poseidon missiles and multiple independently
targeted reentry vehicle (MIRV) warheads, and (3) an armada
of strategic bombers capable of inflicting a third round of
overkill from the air. The new dimension in mass destruction, the MIRV is in the process of development, and the
Nixon administration has launched its limited antiballistic
missile system (Safeguard), designed chiefly to buttress the
United States' power to strike back in the event of a nuclear
attack.

No one with a high regard for human freedom wants to
see the United States disarm unilaterally. If reciprocal limitation of arms proves impossible, we would be courting suicide
to let Moscow or Peking get far ahead in the arms race. But
that danger can be seen only on a remote horizon, while the
risks of overweening extension of our own military reach,
with the result of constantly provoking the arms race that we

[9] Address at Florissant, Missouri, July 4, 1970.

pretend to deplore, are immediately evident in any objective survey of the world around us. The truth is that we have been guilty of a colossal feat of self-deception. In the past most of us seem to have taken it for granted that we ought to have far greater military strength than any other power because we are a peaceful democratic people who can be trusted to use it wisely. But that concept has undergone a damaging upset in Vietnam. A vast number of our friends abroad and disillusioned people at home, including the United States Senate, now see the war in Southeast Asia as a product of excessive reliance on military solutions for complex political problems.

To see ourselves in perspective, we must add overwhelming industrial, economic, financial, and scientific power to our military stature. The American economy produced a gross national product of $861 billion in 1968 compared to $430 billion for the Soviet Union, $142 billion for Japan, $132 billion for the German Federal Republic, $115 billion for France, $103 billion for Britain, and an estimated $40.5 billion for India. Add all the estimated gross national product of the Warsaw Pact countries to that of the Soviet Union and it still falls more than $300 billion short of the U.S. total, to say nothing of our allies in the North Atlantic Alliance and elsewhere.

Myron L. Koenig of the Foreign Service Institute gives us a vivid picture of our relationship to the remainder of the world in his statistics for an imaginary square mile of territory that he calls Worldville. On these 640 acres he places an imaginary 1000 adults — a representative cross section of the three billion persons who inhabit the earth. Only 60 of the 1000 are Americans, and they live on only 16 of the 640 acres. Yet these Americans receive 50 per cent of all the income distributed in any twelve-month period, with the remaining 50 per cent divided, again very unevenly, among the other 940 residents of Worldville. Three fourths of the inhabitants are constantly plagued by hunger, poverty, disease, and fear. An American of average economic status would have seventeen times the personal possessions of the average non-American. The 60 Americans have a life expectancy of 70 years, the 940 others a life expectancy of less than 40 years.

If all other irritants could be removed, these enormous economic and scientific advantages that Americans enjoy would remain a cause of resentment in other parts of the world. They encourage all the suspicion and distrust that is customarily directed at the big mansion on the hill in a poor neighborhood. Our relations with the rest of the world are thus likely to be difficult in any circumstances. When the rich man on the hill takes it upon himself to build a formidable military establishment, to flaunt his power over other people, to insist on policing the community without even consulting his most influential neighbors, and to dictate many decisions that ought to be the result of candid discussion and common consent, he is inviting trouble — the more so in a revolutionary age when newly emerging nations and the deprived masses everywhere are less interested in ideological controversies than in relief from their poverty.

We face the task, therefore, not merely of liquidating our mistakes, but also of reexamining the easy assumption that we can keep the world on the straight and narrow because our motives are good. When we have joined in genuine collective defense arrangements, such as the North Atlantic Treaty Organization, the results have been highly salutary and gratifying. But our unsustainable commitments beyond the areas of our direct national interests and our adventuring as a sort of lone-wolf policeman in remote areas of the world may have contributed more to instability and war than to freedom and peace. Even if it could be shown that one over-

whelmingly powerful country had been both wise and mag-
nanimous in imposing its will upon lesser powers, they still
wouldn't like it, for reasons that our own founding fathers
well understood.

In some degree President Lyndon B. Johnson recognized
the necessity of pulling back from this superpower complex
when he stopped the bombing in North Vietnam and announced that he would not seek reelection in 1968. The first
year of the Nixon administration brought further progress in
the same direction. Before the new regime was organized the
man who was to become the chief architect of its foreign
policy, Henry A. Kissinger, was saying that the most profound
challenge to American policy-makers would be to "develop
some concept of order in a world which is bipolar militarily
but multipolar politically." Mr. Kissinger, who was then
director of the Defense Studies Program at Harvard University, went on to say that "the United States is no longer in
a position to operate programs globally; it has to encourage
them. It can no longer impose its preferred solution; it must
seek to evoke it." [10] Some months later this idea began to
blossom in slightly modified colors as the policy of the
"lowered profile" and the "less strident voice."

The first specific expression of this policy came in the so-
called Nixon Doctrine outlined at Guam. The central thesis,
as later spread on the record, was "that the United States
will participate in the defense and development of allies and
friends, but that America cannot — and will not — conceive
all the plans, design *all* the programs, execute *all* the decisions and undertake *all* the defense of the free nations of the
world. We will help where it makes a real difference and is
considered in our interest." [11] Although the policy was spe-

[10] From Kissinger's chapter, "Central Issues of American Foreign Policy," in
Agenda for the Nation (Washington: Brookings Institution, 1968), p. 612.
[11] "United States Foreign Policy for the 1970's," President Nixon's report to
Congress, February 18, 1970, p. 5.

cifically aimed at Vietnam, its application was clearly intended to be general.

As the Nixon Doctrine was conceived in the planning stage, before it was tested against the stubborn realities of international life, it embraced four principal elements: First, the administration would "try to move from stalemated confrontations to active negotiations on outstanding issues with the Soviet Union and others." Second, it would encourage regional organizations in which other developed nations would "assume greater responsibilities for leadership and initiative in the affairs of the major regions of the world." Third, we would "lower our voice and our visibility on the world stage," seeking "a more moderate dialogue and a greater degree of partnership with our friends and allies." Fourth, we would continue to respect our treaty obligations and not withdraw from the international scene.[12] Spokesmen for the administration indicated that it had little choice in the matter — that circumstances confronting the nation in 1969 virtually compelled a pullback from the predominant American position of the 1960s.

From the beginning, however, there were some disquieting notes in the lowered voice from Washington. One of them came in the first "state-of-the-world" message ever sent to Congress by a President. In discussing the United States' policies vis-à-vis Asia, Nixon seemed to take on an enormous new obligation that could nowhere be found in our treaties and commitments. "We shall provide a shield," he said, "if a nuclear power threatens the freedom of a nation allied with us, or of a nation whose survival we consider vital to our security and the security of the region as a whole." [13] Since he was discussing American policy in Asia and the Pacific and

---

[12] Secretary of State William P. Rogers before a Conference for Editors and Broadcasters, January 15, 1970.
[13] "United States Foreign Policy for the 1970's," p. 41.

had pointedly emphasized that "we are a Pacific power," he seemed to be offering Asian nations a fresh guarantee of American protection against the Soviet Union and China, whether or not existing treaties require it. Providing a shield for any nation whose survival is vital to the security of the region as a whole is a mammoth undertaking. The pledge seemed to take the White House back into the business of policeman on a grand scale, with the President making the rules and calling all the shots as he might see them after an emergency had arisen.

Other serious questions arose as to the extent of the administration's retreat from globalism when the President ordered the invasion of the sanctuaries that the North Vietnamese were maintaining in Cambodia and Laos to aid the prosecution of its war against South Vietnam. A special chapter will be devoted to the invasions of the sanctuaries. For our purposes here it is enough to note that the net effect of these operations was to widen a war that was supposed to be in the process of liquidation. Nixon sought to justify his decisions by arguing that the capture of enormous quantities of ammunition and other war supplies would cripple the enemy and thus make possible faster withdrawal of American troops. The fact remains, however, that the war in Southeast Asia assumed new dimensions, at least temporarily, when the Cambodian and Laotian borders were crossed. The Cambodian operation turned out to be, not merely a cleanup of the sanctuaries, but also a means of aiding the new Cambodian government of Premier Lon Nol. As American ground forces were being withdrawn, the State Department acknowledged that United States planes were interdicting supply lines and communications, so as to protect American troops in South Vietnam, and in the process were aiding the Cambodian government in its fight against the Viet Cong and the North Vietnamese deep within Cambodia. As in Laos some years before, air operations originally intended to support the American troops in Vietnam soon evolved into participation in the war for control of Cambodia itself. To that extent, the United States expanded its role of policeman in Southeast Asia at a time when it was supposedly relinquishing that role. It was the sudden decision of the President to make a bold new strike involving another country — a decision taken, incidentally, entirely on his own responsibility, without the consent or even the knowledge of Congress — which befogged the new image of the U.S.A. that the administration had previously attempted to set up.

So nagging questions of great moment once more edge to the fore. Has the United States, which looks upon itself as the savior of the free world, become a menace to other nations and peoples without realizing it? Has our preoccupation with our own national security undermined the basis on which peace and stability must rest in a multipolar world? In our overweening zeal to beat the Communists in every race, have we lost the confidence and good will of our best friends?

The whole picture of our ubiquitous presence, our military overkill, and our interventions in countries where we have only tangential interests needs to be critically examined. The disillusionment that is rampant within our own country is closely related to the gulf between American ideals and American performance on the international scene. One observer goes so far as to say that "the Asian war is now becoming our second civil war" and that "ARVN and NLF soldiers are just one set of participants in a broader struggle that also pits American against American." [14] In our big push to become the most secure nation on earth, in addition to being the richest and strongest, we have lost much of the perspective we once had. America the cradle of democracy,

[14] Kevin P. Phillips in the *Washington Post*, June 26, 1970, p. A15.

the champion of freedom, and the hope of the oppressed is in danger of becoming America the inveterate meddler, the armored giant, and the insensitive prodigal on the international scene.

In the chapters that follow an attempt will be made to outline the extent of these aberrations and to examine the problems they have laid at our door.

II

Twentieth-Century Hercules

No NATION since the days of ancient Rome has maintained a military presence in the world comparable to that of the United States in the 1950s and 1960s. Great Britain in her palmiest era was mistress of the seas and controlled a far-flung empire from Hong Kong and Singapore to Gibraltar and the West Indies. But she never stood astride the globe in the dominant posture that the United States assumed after World War II. The sudden emergence of the United States from its pre-1917 isolation to a global role during the next two generations is one of the most striking events of world history.

Before this dramatic emergence of the U.S.A., Britain had come nearer than any other modern power to making its influence felt throughout the world. In addition to their facilities at Hong Kong and Singapore, the British maintained bases in India, the Persian Gulf, Iraq, Suez, Kenya, South Africa, and Malta. Lesser way stations, colonies, and servicing facilities for the British Navy could be found in many other parts of the world. Taken all together, however, they are not comparable to the 450 major bases and 2208 minor bases that the American military forces maintained abroad in 1961. Since 1961 the United States has closed a substantial number of its military installations in other countries, but the total is still rather staggering. With Britain giving up most of its bases east of Suez, and with the Soviet Union relying on other means of making its power felt, the United States is the only nation that presumes to maintain a formidable array of military bases far from its own shores. Some of these bases are, of course, a legacy from World War II. The base-building fever began with President Franklin D. Roosevelt's exchange of fifty destroyers for lease rights from the United Kingdom to permit the building of bases in Bermuda, Canada, and the British West Indies. After the war it was necessary to establish new bases in Germany and Japan for the occupying forces, and, with the development of NATO and SEATO, bases burgeoned in many European and Asian countries. The wars in Korea and Vietnam brought further base-building spurts, and military facilities proliferated in other parts of the world because the Pentagon thought they might be useful in meeting potential Communist threats.

It is interesting to note how a military base for United States use in another country comes into being. The initiative usually comes from a theater commander who observes that an Army, Navy, or Air Force base would be useful in carrying out his assignment. He first presents his request, through proper channels, to the Joint Chiefs of Staff and the secretary of defense. If these officials agree that there is a need for an American military presence in the country in question or for an operational base to support our national commitments, the secretary carries the problem to the National Security Council. Here it probably comes to the attention of the President for the first time, as he customarily presides over the NSC. That body addresses itself to the question of whether a base at the spot recommended is a national requirement. If its decision is in the affirmative, the State Department takes over the chore of negotiating with the host country for the right to build the base and for a site on which to locate it.

In effect the secretary of state becomes a sort of errand boy for the Pentagon, the NSC, and of course the President, in carrying out the details. The secretary of state is, to be sure, a member of the National Security Council, but he is likely to be at a serious disadvantage in challenging any project of this kind that goes into the NSC with the united backing of the secretary of defense and the Joint Chiefs. So the question is likely to be decided on its military merits, with relatively little attention to diplomatic problems and the overall psychological effect of seeming to make the world a sort of American armed camp.

Congress doesn't get into the decision-making process until the question of money to build the base arises. Members of the Senate Foreign Relations Committee and the House Foreign Affairs Committee are usually informed about the project during the planning and development process, but only as a courtesy. Congress as a body gets no opportunity to pass judgment on the wisdom or necessity of the project until the decision has been made at the Pentagon and the White House. Then, if money is needed for the proposed installation, a line item is inserted in an appropriations bill providing the authorization as well as the funds. In wartime, however, the construction may already be under way before Congress has a chance to make a decision, with financing supplied from the President's contingency fund. Even in peacetime the President customarily has a contingency fund of around $40 million that can be used for this purpose, with only the proviso that he report any draft upon it for unauthorized foreign bases. As a practical matter, therefore, Congress cannot stop the construction of a military base abroad without raising a hullabaloo, risking the displeasure of the President, overruling the military, and seeming to disregard the country's vital interests, possibly in an emergency. So the cards are all stacked against interference with the wishes of the Pentagon and against any comprehensive national discussion of the larger issue of our posture before the world.

For many years before the Vietnam tragedy worked its disillusionment, Congress was little disposed to question military judgments in any matter. The military was given almost a free hand. It is scarcely surprising that American military bases were spread over 2,561,279 acres of land in thirty-three foreign countries. In 1969 the American military personnel assigned to these bases numbered 1,074,983 and the United States civilians 26,071. They had with them 347,452 dependents, and the bases employed 256,383 foreign nationals, making a grand total of 1,704,889. The Pentagon puts the cost of operating these bases, including the ones in Southeast Asia, at $13.5 billion per year. Taken as a whole, it is a truly staggering commitment to the cause of maintaining peace in the world — a commitment that is often seen abroad in terms of imperialism rather than peace. It is disillusioning if not shocking that our policy-makers seem never to have seriously addressed themselves to the question of whether the miscellaneous proliferation of military installations abroad has done more harm than good so far as our basic national interests are concerned.

From the military viewpoint, all of these bases are essential to our national security. Bases are not an end in and of themselves. They are designed, so the military argument runs, to support "our current strategy of forward defense, collective security, and flexible response." Underlying this "strategy of forward defense" is the idea that aggression and war, if they must come, can be kept far from our shores. If Communism can be stopped in Korea, Vietnam, Laos, and Thailand, we are less likely to have to stop it in Hawaii, Maine, or California. To the military, that is not only a plausible argument but also an unanswerable one. Everyone wants to avoid war or at least to escape its tragic consequences, and if a proliferation of military bases abroad can accomplish this, why should anyone object? They are said to be merely a part of the resources that the Pentagon buys in the interests of peace and security.

Approaching the question from a slightly different angle, the bases are said not to determine our commitments abroad but merely to reflect the specific military requirements of collective security. If the United States intervenes in some distant land threatened by Communism or chaos, it is not because it may have a base there but because it wishes to protect certain fundamental national interests. Yet it seems obvious that the national interest is changed somewhat by reason of the fact of having bases in the country in question. Whether so intended or not, the base becomes a sort of guarantee of the host country's integrity and independence. It creates a relationship that did not exist before regardless of what the mutual defense treaty between the two countries may say, and in some respects it undercuts collective security.

In the case of Vietnam and Thailand, for example, neither Britain nor France deemed it essential to build military bases in those countries to carry out their obligations under the SEATO Treaty. They were as much bound to act against aggression in Southeast Asia as the United States was, but the go-it-alone policy in Washington gave the other major SEATO powers an excellent excuse for doing nothing. The bases built on foreign soil by one of the parties to the alliance became an unmistakable symbol of its unilateral policy. The Pentagon seemed more interested in carrying out its "strategy of forward defense" than in the promotion of regional defense systems and long-range security considerations.

Herein lies the most critical weakness in the policy that has been followed. American bases have been scattered over the globe in an extremely ambitious effort to safeguard western civilization. Senator Stuart Symington, who served as secretary of the Air Force in the Truman administration, once declared, with some exaggeration, that "The only place in the world where you don't see the American military is Israel." [1] If security consisted only in preparations to fight, our national safety would seem to be guaranteed for the indefinite future. But an excess of military preparation can undercut the psychology of peace that the United States is otherwise laboring so hard to cultivate. Both our friends and our enemies abroad would rather count our bases than listen to our oratory about peaceful intentions. It is not surprising that they are skeptical about an American peace dictated by more than a million GIs operating from more than 2000 military bases in thirty-three countries at a cost of approximately $13.5 billion a year. Viewed in its broadest outlines, the policy unquestionably hints that official Washington regards the world as its oyster.

Many individual bases and groups of bases must be exempted from this criticism. More than 140 of the "Major Military Installations and Activities Outside the United States" listed by the Defense Department in 1968 were in West Germany, all Army facilities except for eight Air Force bases. Included in the list were many barracks, hospitals, ammunition and supply depots, air fields, and training areas. Most of the 315,000 Americans in uniform who were in Europe at the beginning of 1970, along with 235,000 dependents, were stationed on these bases. They are the heart of the American contribution to NATO. About 20 per cent of the air bases are used jointly with German forces. By 1970 West Germany had taken over most of its own ground and air defenses. The American air bases in that country are maintained chiefly for tactical support of the NATO defense system and for the transportation of troops and supplies in case of emergency.

These American bases remain in Europe a quarter cen-

[1] Interview with Ward Just in the *Washington Post*, April 7, 1969, p. A20.

tury after the end of World War II at the urgent request of the West German government and the other NATO powers as a symbol of the collective defense that is still essential to the security of Europe. While their number has been reduced in recent years and will doubtless be further cut back as tensions ease and the European powers take over a larger share of their defense responsibilities, it is not these bases that are giving the United States a bad name in world opinion.

The same may be said of the thirteen major bases maintained in Britain by the United States Navy and Air Force. Seven of the air fields have been used jointly by American pilots and the Royal Air Force. The Navy maintains administrative units and naval support activity in London and a naval installation at Greenock, Scotland. It has communications stations in Londonderry, Ireland, and Edzell, Scotland. The nuclear submarine tender maintained at Holy Loch, Scotland, is not even mentioned in the list of bases. The air bases are used largely for fighter planes that are part of the NATO defense system and for air-transport service. The 24,000 Americans with air and naval units in Britain during the late 1960s produced some of the problems that are experienced wherever military personnel are stationed abroad, but these were minor as measured against the great advantages of the NATO shield. The Europeans are generally far more conscious of the value of NATO and of the necessity of active American participation in it than are people living greater distances from the Soviet armies.

In Italy too the nine American bases are closely tied in with NATO. A South Europe Tactical Air Facilities Headquarters is maintained at Verona, with supporting groups, depots, and supplies in Vincenza and Livorno. The Navy has a hospital and an administrative staff in Naples and naval air facilities in Sicily. A fighter squadron at the Aviano

AFB, near Roveredo in Piano, contributes to the air defense of northern Italy. A small missile force is also maintained at Vincenza.

The southern wing of NATO has a formidable naval force consisting of British, Italian, Greek, and Turkish ships as well as vessels from the United States 6th Fleet, which has docking facilities at Gaeta, just north of Naples. In an emergency the 6th Fleet would become the striking and support force for the NATO command in southern Europe. Although the French are no longer direct participants in the NATO military operations, they maintain a liaison office at the NATO headquarters in Naples. In 1968 the alarm that was felt over the build-up of Soviet ships in the Mediterranean led to the creation of Maritime Air Forces, South Europe, consisting of United States, United Kingdom, and Italian units. Its purpose is to locate potential enemy submarines, keep them under surveillance, and attack them when and if it should become necessary.

Rounding out the bases that support NATO, there is a small installation in Amsterdam that provides logistical aid. In Greece the United States Navy maintains a communications station at Néa Mákri, and the Air Force makes use of the Athenai Airport for transporting men, equipment, and supplies into Greece. On the island of Crete the Iraklion Air Station near Gournes has considerable importance as the only logistics support base in a large sea area. In the Atlantic, Lajes Field in the Azores affords opportunity for midocean refueling and other contingencies (a less significant function since the development of longer-range planes) and serves as home base for an antisubmarine patrol. The Navy's bases in the Bahamas are devoted chiefly to underwater weapons research and tracking operations for the space program. Bermuda provides facilities for underwater research and logistics support at Southampton parish and Sandy's parish.

Use of the Kindley Air Force Base at St. George, Bermuda, dwindled to a point where the Air Force relinquished it to the Navy in 1970 for use in antisubmarine activities. The one United States military establishment in Canada, Goose Air Base near St. Anthony, supports the Distant Early Warning or DEW line radar system and would provide air defense in case of necessity. Thule Air Base in Greenland is also tied in with the DEW line and our air defenses in the arctic region. Sondrestrom Air Base on Greenland is a way station for the airlift system — a station that has lost some of its utility as the range of military planes has been lengthened. The naval station at Keflavik, Iceland, is used largely by the antisubmarine air patrol.

Only two groups of bases outside the United States are of primary importance in defense of the Western Hemisphere — those in the Panama Canal Zone and in Guantánamo Bay, Cuba. The Army, Navy, and Air Force all have bases in the Canal Zone. They provide, first of all, protection for the vital waterway that links the Atlantic and Pacific Oceans. In the background is a thinly veiled secondary purpose — maintenance of peace in the Caribbean tinderbox. A substantial amount of training is also carried on in the Canal Zone, and this assumed larger proportions when the Panama jungle proved to be an ideal spot for the training of guerrillas to fight in Southeast Asia.

Guantánamo is the Navy's main operating base in the Caribbean. It has a naval hospital, public works center, supply depot, and naval air station in addition to the base for naval operations. Like the Canal Zone bases, Guantánamo is also closely related to the United States' objectives in Latin America, and it is reasonable to assume that it would be kept in lusty condition, even if it served no military function, because it is an embarrassment to the Castro regime at Havana. The picture of military might in the Caribbean is

completed with the bases in the Commonwealth of Puerto
Rico, which, at this point at least, is still United States territory. Ramey Air Base is a major center of Strategic Air
Command operations, and Roosevelt Roads is an operations
and training base for the Navy. Puerto Rico's weather makes
it a favorite spot for the training of pilots. Chaguaramas
Naval Station in Trinidad, once manned by 200 Americans,
was given up in 1967 on the ground that it was no longer
necessary.

As we move away from the NATO and Pan American
mutual-defense systems, the arguments for continued maintenance of great centers of American power become more
tenuous. Most of the American bases in Asia are a hangover
from the wars we have fought there. From the military viewpoint, they remain essential for the discouragement of future
aggression and for the suppression of Communist uprisings
should they occur. But how far does the United States intend
to go in keeping the peace in distant lands where we are
certain to be suspected of imperialistic intentions? Despite
the pulling back from some ultrasensitive places, the array
of American bases still in use is ample evidence of our excessive globalism.

Japan and Okinawa provide formidable bastions in the
Far East. In the days before Pearl Harbor, Japan's own
military power dominated Asia; now American forces based
on Japan are in control. The Army has developed in Japan
an immense complex of depots, ammunition storage facilities,
training stations, and so forth. That country is the major
stop on the airlift functioning between the United States and
other Asian nations. Troops and supplies for Korea, Vietnam, and other places flow through the Japanese bases.
Hospitals to care for wounded GIs in Vietnam also operate in
safety in Japan. In return the American Air Force and Navy
defend Japan from any possible outside attack. American air

units rotate between Japan and Korea. The Navy too is heavily represented in Japanese waters. The great naval base at Sasebo is supplemented by many other facilities for the repair and overhauling of ships and aircraft. Antisubmarine forces operate out of Yokosuka and Sasebo. Marine fighters also have their place in a formidable array of forces.

On Okinawa the Air Force operates a big SAC and air-defense base (Kadena), the Navy has an antisubmarine base at Naha, and these are supplemented by an almost staggering array of camps, training areas, ammunition depots, and other military installations. We shall have a closer look at this center of military might in the chapter on Japan and Okinawa. For the moment it is sufficient to note the extent to which American military power has supplanted that of Japan, using the soil and some of the facilities of our former enemy.

On Taiwan the United States maintains an Air Force base at Chiayi largely to give administrative support to the Chinese Nationalist forces, a communications center, and a naval administrative and training base. The seven Air Force bases in Thailand were built from 1966 to 1968 primarily for support of the American and South Vietnamese forces in the war against the invading North Vietnamese. But Pentagon spokesmen also confess that they were built in part for the broader purpose of defending Southeast Asia as a whole. They stand as a symbol of the go-it-alone attitude of the Johnson administration in carrying out the provisions of the SEATO Treaty.

The fifty-five American bases in South Korea house the three American divisions that are maintained there, together with their weapons, equipment, supplies, and ammunition. Two Air Force bases at Kunsan and Song Tan are used by fighter squadrons in support of the ground troops. Here too the Navy carries on antisubmarine operations, on the sea and in the air, and amphibious activities. In Vietnam, of course, the sixteen major bases built by all three of the American armed services are directly related to prosecution of the war.

All these bases in the Far East have been added to what the United States maintains in the Philippines, a former possession, and Guam, where this country has had a base since 1898. The fleet operating base at the Philippines' Subic Bay, together with the Cubi Point complex, has cost American taxpayers $215 million. Included are ship-repair facilities, a naval air station, supply depot, magazine, public works center, and hospital. Clark Air Base at Angeles on the island of Luzon serves the Strategic Air Command and is an important link in the Pentagon's airlift network. On Guam a complex of bases greatly strengthens the American military position in the Western Pacific. The Navy's large operating base for fleet units on Guam is supported by a ship-repair station, a naval communications station, a magazine, public works center, supply depot, hospital, and naval air stations at Agana and on the island of Saipan. Naval ammunition storage and antisubmarine activities are important parts of the operations here, and Andersen Air Force Base provides another unit in the airlift system. Two bases in the Marshall Islands, on Kwajalein and Eniwetok, are used largely for research and development in the air defense field. Midway has a naval communications station and an airstrip.

The formidable array of American bases overseas is rounded out by various special arrangements that are not related to any particular treaty or regional defense system but reflect the pervasive Pentagon yearning for power in potentially useful places. Foremost among these are the eight bases in Spain. A separate chapter will be devoted to the problems resulting from this relationship. At this point it is sufficient to note that the convenience of operating air surveillance from Spain and of allowing stopovers by craft flying between the United States and the Mediterranean overcame in the minds of American officials the disadvantages of a link with the Franco regime in Madrid. There are undoubtedly some pluses from the American viewpoint in the naval station at Rota which supports a fleet of Polaris submarines carrying nuclear weapons ready to be fired at sea as a defense against any possible nuclear attack, but the very fact that the United States tried to hire military bases on foreign soil apart from any logical mutual defense system led to formidable complications. At the beginning of 1970, Moron Air Base was in mothballs and the base at Zaragoza had been reduced to standby status, but both could be quickly reactivated in case of need.

Quite a number of foreign bases have proven to be so troublesome in their international repercussions that no alternative to closing them was left. Probably the most notable one in this category is the Peshawar electronic "spy base" in Pakistan, near the Khyber Pass where more than 3000 Americans were stationed at one time. Undoubtedly Peshawar was a useful listening post close to China and not far from the Soviet Union. It has been described as "a highly sophisticated and computerized listening post to eavesdrop on electronic communications." [2] But when it became associated with Francis Gary Powers' U-2 reconnaissance flight that ended disastrously in the Soviet Union in 1960 — Powers had refueled at Peshawar — it was so embarrassing to the Pakistani that they insisted on closing it as soon as they could legally do so. Another factor was the cutoff of American aid to Pakistan in 1965 as a result of the twenty-two-day war with India. Pakistan then turned to China and the Soviet Union for arms and could no longer logically aid

[2] William J. Coughlin in the *Washington Post*, April 10, 1969, p. A15.

American cold war activities, although Pakistan remained a member of the SEATO alliance.

Other special-purpose bases that cost American taxpayers more than $375 million were in Morocco and had to be given up partly because of hostility within that country. An additional reason was the phasing out of the B–47 bomber in favor of the longer-range B–52s operating from bases within the United States, but the growing friction between the two countries would probably have resulted in termination of the bases agreement in any event. One of the huge American bases — Nouaceur — was transformed into a civil airport by the Moroccan government. The only remnant of the American installations left is a communications station.

Rising nationalism in Libya forced the closing of the $100 million, 2100-acre Wheelus Air Base in that country in 1970. The Pentagon regarded it as a serious loss because of the excellent weather in Libya for flight training and bombing practice. But why should a proud and independent country in North Africa provide training grounds for American pilots? Several incidents contributed to the Libyan decision not to renew the lease for Wheelus, including the smuggling of a Libyan Jew out of the base on a United Air Force plane bound for Malta. But the chief cause may well have been the fact that Wheelus was a symbol of the offensive idea that Americans are entitled to plant their military bastions anywhere in the world.

Vital listening points are still maintained at Kagnew Station in Ethiopia and at Karamursel in Turkey. The Pentagon does its utmost to discourage visits to them and to suppress any discussion of their function, but their operations are well known to foes as well as friends. However valuable their eavesdropping may be, their potential for poisoning relations between nations is well established. If the United States is to continue operations of this kind, despite the increasingly valuable information it gets from earth satellites and other sources, we must at least recognize the high price we have to pay for such "communications" in terms of international tensions and distrust.

Some other forces besides international friction are contributing to the attrition of the American base system, the foremost of these being economy. The number of United States minor bases abroad was reduced from 2660 in 1961 to 2270 in 1969 and the number of major bases from 452 to 343 in the same period. As of June 30, 1960, 83.1 per cent of the military real property controlled by the Department of Defense, figured on a cost basis, was located in the United States, 3.7 per cent in our possessions and 13.2 per cent in foreign countries. As of June 30, 1968, the domestic portion had increased to 84.4 per cent; the figure for our possessions remained the same; and the bases in foreign countries accounted for 11.9 per cent.[3] Lest anyone suppose from this comparison that the land used by the American military forces in other countries is an insignificant area, it is well to remember that the larger total of Defense Department land in the U.S.A. exceeds in acreage the entire state of Ohio.

The trimming of our military holdings abroad got a good start when President De Gaulle's coolness toward NATO made it necessary to close 52 major and 174 minor installations in France during 1966 and 1967. The net effect, however, was to shift about 70,000 Americans in uniform from France to American bases in Britain, Belgium, Germany, Italy, and elsewhere. Some fifteen American installations in West Germany have been turned over to German forces during the last few years. In England the Brunting Thorpe and Fairford Air Bases were returned to the Royal Air Force because of the phasing out of the B–47 medium bomber, and

---

[3] "Real and Personal Property of the Department of Defense," report by the Office of the Comptroller, 1968, p. 27.

the Prestwick Airfield in southern Scotland was relinquished to full civilian use because the development of longer-range aircraft and improved refueling techniques made further use of it unnecessary. A USAF fighter unit operating out of Italy's Grossetto Air Base was closed out because of consolidation of activities in the South Europe and Mediterranean areas.

In the Far East, Tainan Air Station was turned back to the Chinese National Air Force because the Matador missile which it had been equipped to handle had become obsolete. The Johnson Air Base was relinquished to the Japanese government after its tactical wing and administrative and supply functions had been moved elsewhere. Under a 1969 agreement about fifty American installations in Japan were scheduled for release, relocation, or conversion, and extensive shifts and readjustments were announced at the close of 1970. The Nixon administration claimed that it had closed a total of sixty-eight foreign military bases and reduced forty-four more, but the withholding of details made it impossible to determine how many of the closings were really significant in terms of our military posture abroad.

No doubt consolidations, economy cutbacks, and closings because of excessive friction abroad will continue. But they reflect an expedient response to changing conditions. It remains to be seen whether any major shift in policy is in the making. The Johnson administration put thirty civilian and military experts to work surveying American bases abroad with a view to recommending a national policy. After ten months of study and 85,000 miles of travel this team, headed by General Robert J. Wood, retired chief of the military-aid program, and Robert McClintock, a senior foreign service officer and former ambassador to Argentina and Lebanon, produced a lengthy report, but it never saw the light of day. When the Nixon administration came in, it launched a series of base studies of its own, using the Wood-McClintock report as a starting point. There is no indication, however, that any of the reports resulting from these efforts will surface for public discussion. Like its predecessors, the Nixon administration is disposed to keep the whole subject close to its chest.

Some details and conclusions from the Wood-McClintock report were leaked to the press, and these seem to coincide with the general trend of Pentagon thinking. Benjamin Welles of the *New York Times* summarized the conclusions as follows:

> There is little likelihood of early or substantial cutbacks in overseas bases as long as the United States intends to honor its treaty commitments.
>
> Even such developments in military technology as the huge C–5A air-cargo plane and nuclear-powered warships do not eliminate the need for substantial numbers of overseas bases and skilled personnel.
>
> To relinquish distant bases and concentrate forces nearer — or even within — the continental United States might cost more than keeping them where they are, on bases long since paid for . . .
>
> The cost of any United States pullback — particularly in the Pacific — would be high if the United States insisted also on retaining the same military capacity in relation to the Communist powers.[4]

If this is an accurate reflection of the views expressed in the report, it is an echo of the philosophy which led to establishment of the bases in the first place. The basic premise seems to be that the United States is committed to the suppression of Communism everywhere outside of China, the Soviet Union and its Eastern European satellites, and such

[4] Benjamin Welles in the *New York Times,* April 9, 1969, p. 1.

places as North Korea and North Vietnam. Far-flung bases are said to be essential to the role in which we have cast ourselves, but Britain and France, with many similar treaty commitments, do not deem it necessary to support a global chain of military bases for that reason. The fact that Washington has insisted on maintaining centers of military power all around the globe is indicative of the go-it-alone thinking that has prevailed here. We adhere to the collective defense arrangements in words, but we maintain bases in thirty countries so as to be prepared to do the job by ourselves.

If the Nixon policies of "partnership" and of "regionalism" mean anything, we should be moving toward systems of regional bases that would not be under the control of any single power. Maybe that is a utopian concept, but the military cannot have it both ways. If our main effort for a peaceful world is to be the maintenance of hundreds of American centers of military power in other lands, it will be a military peace, if any, and the United States will be recognized as a sort of global policeman however vehemently we may decline the role in our intramural thinking and debates. Who ever heard of a good neighbor who maintained an arsenal in every street just in case?

The image of the U.S.A. as the armed rich man of the globe is the more ironic because our military preponderance is designed to protect freedom and democracy. In both theory and practice, violence, dictatorship, and supremacy of the state are associated with Communism. Our basic complaint about Communism is that it tries to impose its will upon people by force and terror. Yet we ourselves construct and maintain the greatest complex of military bastions in all history. However loudly we may proclaim that they are used for defensive purposes only, their presence remains disturbing to many peoples who are less disposed to credit us with righteous intentions.

Official Washington has never been willing to face candidly this negative aspect of our borrowed or leased overseas empire. It has laid great store on the military value of the bases while ignoring the psychological repercussions set in motion in many different parts of the world by the United States' excessive efforts to guarantee its own safety. The time may not be far off, considering the unfavorable reactions in many countries, when the losses we suffer in terms of good will and international trust because of our conspicuous military presence will clearly offset the military advantages of setting up our defense establishments on other countries' soil.

President Nixon came close to recognizing the problem in his message to Congress on foreign policy on February 18, 1970. In emphasizing his bid for partnership in this "era of negotiations," the President said:

> The United States, like any other nation, has interests of its own, and will defend those interests. But any nation today must define its interests with special concern for the interests of others. If some nations define their security in a manner that means insecurity for other nations, then peace is threatened and the security of all is diminished. This obligation is particularly great for the nuclear superpowers on whose decisions the survival of mankind may well depend.

Many countries in and out of the Communist orbit believe that the United States has defined its security in a manner that means insecurity for other nations. The fact that we do not see any such danger from within the protected confines of our military base complex does not mean that it is viewed with equanimity in the minds of other peoples. Their concern becomes the more acute because this most powerful of all nations has been repeatedly involved in wars during recent decades. The only clear way of looking at our exaggerated definition of our security is to ask ourselves whether we would feel insecure if another nuclear power of great resources and military prowess maintained hundreds of military bases scattered around the world, some of them close to our own shores.

The base problem needs to be reexamined, therefore, not only in terms of military needs in the 1970s but also in terms of its psychological impact upon the world in general. We are not likely to be credited with peaceful intentions until the lowering of our military profile in distant lands has gone much further than it did in the first years of the Nixon administration. The Nixon Doctrine calls for helping our friends in their defense efforts and economic development, for joining as partners in regional arrangements, without trying to make all plans and execute all decisions. But it is not likely to be taken very seriously unless we are willing to relinquish a substantial portion of the military trappings now maintained from Taiwan to Spain.

What we do with these bases may well be the key to our future role in helping to keep the peace.

III

Collective Defense Undermined

THE FIRST QUESTION that must be asked about our sprawling commitments all over the globe is why collective defense agreements have brought so little collective action. There is, of course, a notable exception in NATO. From its inception NATO has been predominantly a cooperative venture. Although the American presence has often loomed too large, we have not presumed to ignore our NATO allies and go it alone in Europe. In most instances common policies have been hammered out in the NATO Council, and a sufficiently impressive defense organization has been maintained to avoid the necessity of testing its strength in major combat. After two decades the pledge that each country would react to an attack on any member of the alliance as if the attack were against itself still remains intact. NATO is a highly creditable example of collective defense.

The same can scarcely be said for various other collective defense arrangements to which the United States adheres. The two major systems, aside from NATO, are the Organization of American States, which functions in the Western Hemisphere, and the Southeast Asia Treaty Organization. Both are built on the principle of regionalism. Both are designed to provide security without big-power domination of, or dictation to, the smaller members of the alliance. Yet in both of these systems, when crises have arisen, the United States has intervened on a unilateral basis almost as if no collective security had been contemplated.

The first notable example is the Bay of Pigs. The United States had good reason to be irritated and troubled when Fidel Castro, having upset a corrupt and tottering government in Cuba, allied his revolution with international Communism. Cuba thereby became a thorn in the flesh of all the American republics, but not, as Senator J. William Fulbright once said, "a dagger in the heart." [1] The Americas had agreed among themselves how they would deal with a situation of this kind. The Inter-American Treaty of Reciprocal Assistance signed at Rio de Janeiro in 1947 established the principle that "an armed attack by any State against an American State shall be considered as an attack against all the American States." Collective measures against such an attack were to be taken through the Organ of Consultation. The treaty then went on to provide in Article 6:

> If the inviolability or the integrity of the territory or the sovereignty or political independence of any American State should be affected by an aggression which is not an armed attack or by an extra-continental or intra-continental conflict, or by any other fact or situation that might endanger the peace of America, the Organ of Consultation shall meet immediately in order to agree on the measures which must be taken in case of aggression to assist the victim of the aggression or, in any case, the measures which should be taken for the common defense and for the maintenance of the peace and security of the Continent.[2]

[1] Arthur M. Schlesinger, Jr., *A Thousand Days: John F. Kennedy in the White House* (Boston: Houghton Mifflin, 1965), p. 251.
[2] *Legislation on Foreign Relations with Explanatory Notes,* printed for use of the Senate Foreign Relations Committee and House Foreign Affairs Committee (Washington: Government Printing Office, 1968), p. 557.

The language could not be much clearer if it had been specifically tailored to the Cuban situation. In case of a subversive threat arising within the Pan American family the action to be taken would be agreed upon within the Organ of Consultation. This law of the American states was further buttressed and spelled out in the Charter of the Organization of American States which was approved at Bogotá in 1948. The charter lays down four cardinal principles which were the price that had to be paid to get a common hemispheric defense policy:

(1) "Each State has the right to develop its cultural, political, and economic life freely and naturally."

(2) "The American States bind themselves in their international relations not to have recourse to the use of force, except in the case of self-defense . . ."

(3) "The territory of a State is inviolable; it may not be the object, even temporarily, of military occupation or of other measures of force taken by another State, directly or indirectly, on any grounds whatever."

(4) "No State or group of States has the right to intervene, directly or indirectly, for any reason whatever, in the internal or external affairs of any other State. The foregoing principle prohibits not only armed force but also any other form of interference or attempted threat against the personality of the State or against its political, economic and cultural elements."

History bears ample witness that these stern and unequivocal rules were aimed primarily and almost solely against the United States because of the role this country had played as protector, schoolmaster, and policeman of the hemisphere until the policy of Theodore Roosevelt was reversed by Franklin D. Roosevelt. By ratifying the treaty the United States bound itself to forgo the big stick and to rely upon peace-keeping measures which the entire OAS could agree upon. That substitution of collective security for the arbitrary abuse of national power was widely hailed in both hemispheres as a great contribution to a peaceful world.

John F. Kennedy fully recognized the validity and rightness of this principle when he began to grapple with the Cuban problem in the 1960 campaign. "We can't do anything except through the OAS," he said at Hyannis Port, "and most of the members of the OAS don't want to do anything at all." [3] A few weeks later, however, he talked about strengthening the Cuban "fighters for freedom," and shortly after the election he learned that the Central Intelligence Agency was training a Cuban brigade in Guatemala for what had been originally designed as a guerrilla infiltration of Cuba. At first the new President appeared to be wary of the proposed venture. He requested the Defense Department to examine the CIA's military plan and the State Department to work up a program for isolation and containment of Cuba by action of the OAS. Nevertheless, the CIA was given a green light to carry on, with the understanding, first laid down by the Eisenhower administration, that there was to be no direct United States participation. As the weeks passed it became more and more evident that there was no convenient point for checking the avalanche that the CIA had been allowed to unloose, and so the fiasco moved on to its inevitably tragic end that is now so well recorded in American history.

There was some scattered opposition, but no one seemed to take it very seriously. Senator Fulbright, the chairman of the Senate Foreign Relations Committee, vented his fears about the invasion build-up in Guatemala when he was a guest on the President's plane during a flight to Florida late in March, 1960. Later he submitted a memorandum to President Kennedy arguing that a United States maneuver to

[3] Schlesinger, p. 225.

overthrow Castro would violate the spirit and letter of the OAS charter and perhaps federal law. It would provoke worldwide denunciation and create embarrassing problems in the United Nations. "To give this activity even covert support," the senator argued, "is of a piece with the hypocrisy and cynicism for which the United States is constantly denouncing the Soviet Union in the United Nations and elsewhere." [4]

Fulbright was given a chance to make his argument before the President and his chief advisers on the Cuban project on April 4 at the State Department. It was brushed aside by the militants who were eager to strike a blow at Castro even at the risk of upsetting the Pan American defense system. Adlai Stevenson, then ambassador to the United Nations, was also vigorously opposed to the CIA's brainstorm, but he was given no opportunity to make his views known before it was too late. The Secretary of State, Dean Rusk, who should have been weighing the long-range impact of this reckless gesture upon American foreign policy more thoroughly than anyone else, appears to have been sucked in by the flimsy assumption that the end would justify the means. No one had a very clear concept of the project — whether the United States could successfully disown it; whether it would have a chance for success without direct U.S. participation; whether it would stimulate an uprising in Cuba. Yet the biggest question remaining after a decade of probing into the fiasco is why the Kennedy administration supposed that an adventure of so little promise could justify the risk of breaking up the American defense system.

President Kennedy's worries about the outcome were evident in his efforts to confine it to a guerrilla operation instead of an invasion and in his cancellation of the projected second air strike. According to Arthur M. Schlesinger, Jr.,

[4] Schlesinger, p. 251.

Kennedy halted the second strike that had been scheduled from Nicaragua after the Cuban pilots were in the cockpits of B–26 planes waiting for the signal to take off.[5] After a long telephone conversation with Secretary Rusk, the President, who was at his Glen Ora retreat in Virginia, apparently concluded that a second strike from Nicaragua would create international embarrassment, unless the planes could fly or appear to fly from a beachhead already established in Cuba. But it is not clear why a second strike from Nicaragua by Cuban pilots trained by Americans and supplied with American planes and ammunition should be more embarrassing than the first strike from the same place with the same planes and personnel. In those hours of desperation American officialdom appeared to be shadowboxing with mammoth delusions.

President Kennedy is entitled to a good deal of credit for resisting the demands that the United States step in openly and save the venture from humiliating failure. There was a point beyond which he would not go, and he refused to panic in the face of disaster for the sleazy CIA scheme to which his administration had become committed. But in trying to explain the unwillingness of the administration to go all the way its spokesmen talked in terms that are still baffling to anyone who is inclined to call a spade a spade. As the scope of the fiasco filtered through to Washington, Secretary Rusk declared in a press conference: "The American people are entitled to know whether we are intervening in Cuba or intend to do so in the future. The answer to that question is no. What happens in Cuba is for the Cuban people to decide." [6] A few days later President Kennedy told the American Society of Newspaper Editors that unilateral intervention would have violated our traditions and international obligations.

[5] Schlesinger, p. 273.
[6] Schlesinger, p. 275.

Perhaps that was the least costly avenue of retreat, but our Latin American, European, and Asian friends could see only an American plot hatched and nurtured by the CIA and carried out with the aid of American money, equipment, and military training. As the bitter and disillusioned Cuban émigrés pointed out, the men dying on the beaches were Cuban but the planning, the training, the command, the timing, and the decision to go ahead were all American. A great nation that had won world applause for its previous contributions to a hemispheric peace system had sullied its image by secretly undercutting its own principles, and that fact could not be changed by calling it nonintervention.

It would be heartening to record that the Bay of Pigs expedition was an inexplicable aberration in American foreign policy — that the shock the country suffered on that occasion brought a new understanding of our hemispheric commitments and a national resolve not to tolerate further deviations from genuine collective security in our own back yard. Unfortunately, no such repentance followed the belated acknowledgments of error in the Bay of Pigs affair. Four years later the United States indulged in an even more flagrant disruption of the inter-American system by occupying the Dominican Republic.

Here again impatient pragmatists are inclined to argue that the end justified the means. President Lyndon B. Johnson and the men around him in Washington were extremely fearful of a Communist coup in Santo Domingo. How could the United States tolerate another Castro in the American family of nations? The fear that Communism might gain a new foothold on a second island in the Caribbean was not sufficient to bring forth any positive program for the maintenance of self-government in the Dominican Republic in the days when its political institutions were falling apart. But as fear mounted, along with the chaos in Santo Domingo, President Johnson flipped back to the remedy that Theodore

Roosevelt had used in the bad old days long before the "good neighbor" policy had been written into law. He sent in the Marines.

The trouble that had been brewing in Santo Domingo reached critical dimensions on April 24, 1965. Donald Reid Cabral's junta, which had overthrown the freely elected government of Juan Bosch in September, 1963, had come to a parting of the ways with the Dominican military. The following day Reid resigned after seeking United States intervention and receiving no encouragement. The Dominican Revolutionary Party (PRD), which had supported Bosch, then sought a comeback with Rafael Molina Urena as provisional President pending the return of Bosch. Meanwhile they sought a "United States presence" as a means of easing the transfer of governmental power, but no aid was forthcoming either from Washington or the OAS. When the Bosch forces ignored an ultimatum from the military, naval and air forces began firing at the National Palace. A badly divided country with only a flimsy tradition of self-government thus slipped into a state of civil war.

Some observers of these unfortunate events trace much of the responsibility for what happened to the United States Ambassador, W. Tapley Bennett. The ambassador failed to use his good offices to aid a settlement, out of fear that any such mediation might be criticized as "intervention." His attitude appears to have contributed to the feeling of the Bosch forces that their cause was hopeless, which led Molina Urena and some others to seek asylum in Latin American embassies. With the so-called rebel cause thus leaderless, fears mounted at the American Embassy that the PRD would be, or had been, taken over by the Communists. Bennett cabled Washington that the issue was one between Castroism and its opponents and requested that the antirebel forces be provided with fifty walkie-talkies from the United States Defense Department. Despite the ambassador's qualms about intervention, the United States seemed to be lining up on the side of the military in an effort to prevent the followers of Juan Bosch from taking control.

During the afternoon of April 28 an improvised junta under Colonel Pedro Bartol Benoit asked for American troops as the only means of saving the Dominican Republic from a Communist coup. Washington was unresponsive at the moment but hinted that the decision might be different if Colonel Benoit said that he could not protect American citizens who had been caught in the chaos. So Benoit's request was pitched to a different key — that of protecting American lives — and the Marines were soon on their way to Santo Domingo.[7]

Some danger to foreigners always exists when government breaks down in a country where some elements are known to be hostile. In this instance, however, the concern that was expressed in Washington over the perils facing Americans in Santo Domingo appears to have been largely a pretext. Since no Americans had been killed, the fears for their safety might be generously reckoned at 25 per cent, with the remaining 75 per cent of Washington's worry centered in the possibility that the Dominican Republic might be moving toward Castroism.

Senator Fulbright's study of the Dominican episode as chairman of the Senate Foreign Relations Committee led him to this conclusion:

> The United States intervened in the Dominican Republic for the purpose of preventing the victory of a revolutionary force which was judged to be communist-dominated. On the basis of Ambassador Bennett's messages to Washington, there

[7] J. William Fulbright, *The Arrogance of Power* (New York: Vintage Books, 1966), p. 89.

is no doubt that the fear of communism rather than danger to American lives was his primary or sole reason for recommending military intervention. In fact, no American lives were lost in Santo Domingo until the Marines began exchanging fire with the rebels after April 28; reports of widespread shooting that endangered American lives turned out to be greatly exaggerated.[8]

Incidentally, the landing of Marines at Santo Domingo did not become legitimate because of the "save-American-lives" gloss that Washington attempted to put on it. No doubt that explanation sounded somewhat better at home than intervention to save an unstable Caribbean country from Communism. But the charter of the Organization of American States, by which the United States is bound, along with all the other signatories, forbids the military occupation of any state, even temporarily, "directly or indirectly, on any ground whatever." It is reasonable to assume, moreover, that virtually no one took at face value the official explanation of the incident. The net effect was not to legalize the intervention or to make it less culpable in the eyes of critics around the world but rather to undercut the credibility of the United States and its attachment to the Pan American peace system.

Alberto Lleras Camargo, former President of Colombia, described the reaction in Europe, where he was touring at the time, in these words:

> The general feeling was that a new and openly imperialistic policy in the style of Theodore Roosevelt had been adopted by the White House and that, if there was intervention with Marines in the Hemisphere, against unequivocal standards of law, one could only expect — in Asia, in Africa, and in wherever — new acts of force and, perhaps, the escalation of the cold war to the hot in a very short time . . .[9]

[8] Fulbright, p. 90.
[9] Quoted by Fulbright, p. 85.

When the Johnson administration became convinced that the Dominican Republic was in danger of a Communist coup, it had an obligation to lay the case before the OAS. That is precisely what Article 6 of the Rio Pact calls for. Perhaps the OAS would not have responded as quickly as President Johnson did. It would probably have insisted on deliberations and on some evidence of the alleged Communist menace, which would have been difficult to supply. But this is one of the basic reasons why the statesmen assembled at Rio and Bogotá when the new policy was cemented into international law preferred collective security to unilateral action by the United States. They did not trust the judgment of Washington alone in such matters. A hemispherewide policy of maintaining peace would be possible only if the judgment to intervene in any situation were a collective judgment. When the chips were down, however, this cool and deliberate policy of all the Americas was toppled into the ash can by a President's impetuous conclusion that an amorphous Communist menace had to be stopped.

It is true, of course, that the OAS later took some of the curse off the United States' unilateral intervention by internationalizing the occupying force. Order was restored, and a provisional government was set up and maintained in office until a new president of the Dominican Republic, Joaquin Balaguer, was chosen on June 1, 1966, in what appeared to be a fair and free election. The end result seemed to exonerate the Johnson administration of any imperialistic intent or willful desire to break up the hemispheric peace system. Yet a reservoir of good will and trust built up over a period of thirty years had been virtually drained. The concept of collective security had been dealt a severe blow. The image of the United States as a big power willing to share responsibility in matters touching the security of many nations was very sadly tarnished.

The Bay of Pigs and the intervention in Santo Domingo

are the more regrettable because the Organization of American States does need to be strengthened as an instrument for keeping the peace. It has not functioned as vigorously or as effectively as many of its supporters hoped that it would. The tendency of Washington to go it alone, however, is likely to surround any remedial proposals that may be forthcoming from this country with an aura of suspicion. The United States simply cannot have it both ways. It cannot build a reputation as a trustworthy partner and ally if, when the going gets rough, it flouts its treaty obligations and behaves like an undisciplined imperialist.

The other area in which the United States fostered the principle of collective security but acted alone, or almost alone, is, of course, the Far East. There are some who believe that the SEATO Treaty was designed chiefly to give the President of the United States a free hand in combating aggression in Asia, and several Presidents have used it in that fashion. This interpretation is based on Article IV, paragraph 1, which says that each party recognizes that "aggression by means of armed attack" in the treaty area would endanger its own peace and safety and that each party "will in that event act to meet the common danger in accordance with its constitutional processes." Usually this section of the treaty is attributed to John Foster Dulles, who was secretary of state at the time of its adoption, but he was by no means its sole architect. One of its most eminent sponsors was Prime Minister Winston Churchill of Britain. When Churchill and Anthony Eden visited President Eisenhower in June, 1954, the Prime Minister gave full endorsement to a SEATO, corresponding to NATO, as a means of preventing the Communists from establishing a firm base in the Pacific area.[10] Churchill said that support from Asian countries was para-

[10] Dwight D. Eisenhower, *Mandate for Change, 1953–1956* (Garden City: Doubleday, 1963), p. 368.

mount, but he also suggested that the SEATO allies operate nationally, where possible, thinking chiefly of Britain's twenty-three battalions in Malaya.

The delegates who met in Manila in September, 1954 (they represented Australia, France, New Zealand, Pakistan, the Philippines, Thailand, the United Kingdom, and the United States), did make possible individual responses by separate countries in special circumstances. But this ought to be read in the light of the treaty's underlying purpose "to declare publicly and formally their [the members'] sense of unity" and "to coordinate their efforts for collective defense for the preservation of peace and security." The treaty also set up a council, on which all the members were represented, for consultation on military planning and for the consideration of "matters concerning the implementation of this Treaty."

Since the sponsors were chiefly concerned with Communist subversion, moreover, the heart of the treaty is in a separate provision dealing with that subject. It says that if the territorial integrity, sovereignty, or political independence of any country covered by the treaty "is threatened in any way other than by armed attack or is affected or threatened by any fact or situation which might endanger the peace of the area, the parties shall consult immediately in order to agree on the measures which should be taken for the common defense." [11] Inasmuch as the trouble in Vietnam and Laos began as subversive operations, not from invasions from the outside, action would have been most logically taken under this requirement for immediate consultation.

The history of SEATO does not bear out C. L. Sulzberger's assertion that it was a device conceived by Dulles "to enable the President of the United States, by means of an advance blank check signed by the Congress, to take swift action when and if needed to send military aid to any Southeast Asian

[11] *Legislation on Foreign Relations,* p. 617.

country menaced by aggression." [12] In testifying before the
Senate Foreign Relations Committee in regard to ratification
of the SEATO Treaty, Dulles drew a distinction between
NATO and SEATO and said that the Eisenhower administration had no thought of contributing to an army for defense
of Southeast Asia. On the contrary, he said: "I believe that
if there should be open armed attack in that area the most
effective step would be to strike at the source of aggression
rather than to try to rush American manpower into the area
to try to fight a ground war." However misguided his idea of
bombing the aggressor directly may be in the light of subsequent history in Vietnam, it certainly cannot be said that he
envisaged the kind of ground war that evolved in Vietnam
from 1964 to 1968.

Dulles laid a good deal of emphasis, moreover, on the collective aspects of the treaty. Responding to a question by
Senator Margaret Chase Smith at the hearing, he said:

> Well, article IV, paragraph 2, contemplates that if that situa-
> tion [subversion] arises or threatens, that we should consult
> together immediately in order to agree on measures which
> should be taken. That is an obligation for consultation. It is
> not an obligation for action.[13]

Senator Theodore F. Green asked if the treaty would require the United States to help Southeast Asian governments
put down revolution. Dulles's reply was unequivocal:

> No. If there is a revolutionary movement in Vietnam or
> Thailand, we would consult together as to what to do about it,
> because if that were a subversive movement that was in fact
> propagated by communism, it would be a very grave threat to

[12] *New York Times,* January 9, 1970, p. 32C.
[13] "The Southeast Asia Collective Defense Treaty," hearing before the Committee on Foreign Relations, U.S. Senate, 83rd Cong., 2d sess. (Washington:
Government Printing Office, 1954), p. 25.

us. But we have no undertaking to put it down; all we have is an undertaking to consult together as to what to do about it.[14]

There are sound reasons, of course, for requiring consultation before resorting to military action under a mutual defense treaty. Aside from the necessity of holding the alliance together through consistent habits of cooperation, military intervention in any situation is less likely if several governments have to agree upon it. The entire imbroglio in Vietnam might have been avoided if the United States, Britain, France, and the other SEATO allies had met in 1961 or 1964 and sought a common policy. Indeed, the Eisenhower administration tried to work out a coalition with France and Britain in 1954 to save Indochina from the spread of Communism. The project was abandoned because no consensus could be found. SEATO was then created in the hope that it would provide the cement that would be needed in any future crisis. That hope proved illusory, but the very fact that the big powers remained divided in regard to such a venture should have been a warning signal against one of them undertaking it alone. When President Johnson took the entire burden on American shoulders, without calling any conference of the SEATO powers and with only scattering help from small countries dependent upon American aid, he undercut the whole idea of collective defense in Southeast Asia.

However one looks at it, the policy of going it alone, in spite of collective defense treaties, has proved to be a costly experiment. In terms of good will, good faith, and moral standing in world opinion the cost is truly incalculable, but it is known to be enormous. At its worst, this practice puts the United States in the category of treaty flouter or direct

[14] Ibid., p. 28.

treaty breaker, thus encouraging cynics all over the world to assume that there is no difference between a democratic superpower and the architects of international Communism when their supposed national interests are at stake.

In terms of American lives, resources, and money the cost of the Southeast Asian policeman role is still more staggering. Look at it this way: The North Atlantic Treaty Organization, which is the mainstay of our defense system beyond our own borders, is estimated to cost the American taxpayer from $13 to $15 billion a year. Since it has engaged in no actual fighting, its cost in terms of human lives is negligible. Considering the fact that it has averted a third world war centering in Europe, which so many were predicting for the present generation, NATO must be regarded, on the present record, as a bargain. It stands out as the most powerful testimonial in history for collective security pursued in practice as well as in theory.

Our national experience with SEATO presents a shocking contrast. The federal budget for fiscal 1970 listed military outlays in Southeast Asia as follows: fiscal 1965, $103 million; 1966, $6094 million; 1967, $20,557 million; 1968, $26,839 million; 1969, $29,192 million; 1970, $25,733 million. The grand total, mostly for six years of war in Vietnam, is more than $108.5 billion. To this must be added, of course, the death of more than 45,000 Americans and the wounding of about 300,000 others, making Vietnam the third most costly war in which the United States has participated in terms of human lives. And after the war had been winding down for many months from its 1969 peak thoughtful observers were still debating whether anything of lasting consequence had been accomplished in Vietnam.

It is all very well to say that there is no rational basis for drawing a comparison between Western Europe and Southeast Asia. Much that is possible in the NATO area is quite

unattainable for SEATO. The point of drawing the contrast here is not to suggest that a NATO-type defense system
would have done better in Southeast Asia, for a duplication
of NATO in the Far East would have been literally impossible. The warning that is implicit in the record is against
frittering away the major portion of our defense resources
on a remote area that is not vital to our national interest —
a region of which we have little knowledge and in which the
chance of making western-style democracy prevail is rather
poor. And we might have been saved from doing that if the
United States had been willing to consult and to accept a
collective judgment.

The choice for America is not between isolationism and
international cooperation. It is, rather, between genuine
collective security where that is possible in areas of great importance to us and a bogus kind of collective security that is
only a mask for nationalistic ventures that would not be
countenanced by a sober regional council.

While talking the language of collective security, the
United States, as Ronald Steel has pointed out, "has become
entranced by global interventionism as a means of furthering
her moral purpose." [15] Even if this "benevolent imperialism
of Pax Americana" could be justified in the days when it was
supposed that the whole world was in danger of being horn-
swoggled by international Communism directed from Moscow, the policy is certainly out of date in the seventies. Communism is splintered into quarreling and ever-diverging factions, and it is unmistakably evident that the world of the
1970s has no taste for superpower domination whether it
originates in Moscow or Washington. For better or worse,
the United States is going to have to accommodate itself to
increasing give-and-take in the free world, and the most vital
place for this principle to begin operating is in the councils

[15] Ronald Steel, *Pax Americana* (New York: Viking, 1967), p. 336.

set up to decide whether joint military measures are necessary for the common defense. Only a direct attack on our country or its forces can justify a departure from this policy, and then only on an emergency basis.

It is not enough for a great power dedicated to freedom, justice, and peace to negotiate mutual defense treaties; it must also live by them. The first necessity in the operation of such alliances is that the collective judgments prevail. We cannot have our cake and eat it too. If the United States should continue to break out of the collective harness and act on its own responsibility, because it fears that its allies will not share its passion to set something right, we shall ultimately be left alone in a frantic and futile effort to impose our national will on a highly diversified world. The result would almost certainly be hopeless involvement in wars and conflicts that would undermine our strength and weaken our democratic institutions at home.

Democracy is hard medicine for the powerful to swallow even when they believe in it and habitually preach it. When the power is at hand, it is so much easier to send in the Marines or dispatch a bomber squadron than to argue with allies who never did see completely eye to eye with us anyway. So the challenge of our experience in the 1950s and 1960s is very real. We can follow the NATO precedent, with appropriate adjustments and evolutionary growth, and seek to extend cooperative regional ventures when and where feasible. Or we can multiply the incidents that have convinced many of our friends around the world that the United States is incapable of the self-discipline which makes collective security possible.

The major danger is not that we shall repeat the painful experience of Vietnam, at least not in the near future, but that we shall fail to appreciate the constructive possibilities of really working together with other free peoples. A

Churchillian phrase seems appropriate here. Democracy, he once said, is the worst form of government, except all others. In this age of rampant nationalism and intoxicating super-power for two well-known countries, regional alliances faithfully implemented may be the worst form of defense, except that they are the only form which offers substantial security.

IV

The Hidden War in Laos

THE MOST FANTASTIC VENTURE in our global struggle against
Communism has been the hidden war in Laos. The little
kingdom bordering on China, Burma, Thailand, Cambodia,
and North and South Vietnam is one of the last places in
the world where one would expect a build-up of American
power. It has only three million people, most of them peaceful peasants wanting to be left alone. In 1962 the powers
with interests in Southeast Asia signed an agreement designed
to keep Laos neutral. Yet the United States for many years
carried on secret military operations in that country designed
to protect its independence. Although the motive was a
worthy one and our violation of the neutrality agreement
followed more flagrant violation by the North Vietnamese,
this secret war on the other side of the globe is surely one of
the strangest episodes in our history.

From the beginning the venture was peculiarly a presidential responsibility. Congress had passed legislation under
which military aid was given to Laos and partly concealed
appropriations were voted from year to year. Yet the American involvement progressed from limited aid to active participation in the war in Laos without any detailed knowledge
by Congress of what was going on. And no grant of authority

to commit Americans to fight and die in Laos can be found anywhere. Bits of the story were told from time to time by the press, but the facts were not acknowledged until the Senate Subcommittee on United States Security Agreements and Commitments Abroad published its confidential and heavily censored hearings in 1970. No one who is concerned over the lengths to which executive war-making has been carried in this country can afford to miss this little volume.[1]

There is no indication that our venture in Laos was deliberately planned. After the close of World War II, President Truman helped the French return to Indochina for the purpose of reestablishing their colonies in Laos, Cambodia, and Vietnam, which had been overrun by the Japanese. Many authorities on American foreign policy now think that that action reflected poor judgment — that our national interests would have been better served by leaving the struggle in Southeast Asia strictly to the Southeast Asians. But the country was much concerned at the time over the spread of Communism anywhere in the world. During the Eisenhower administrations the government's fears were usually couched in terms of the domino theory — that if the Communists were allowed to overrun one country in Indochina, the others would almost automatically go down.

President Eisenhower was so worried about the movement of North Vietnamese into Laos during his last weeks in office that he intermeddled broadly to support the anti-Communist government headed by Boun Oum. He approved the use of Thai and American aircraft in Laos because of the sorties the Russians were flying in support of the Pathet Lao. "We cannot let Laos fall to the Communists," he told a group of

[1] "United States Security Agreements and Commitments Abroad: Kingdom of Laos," hearings before the Subcommittee on United States Security Agreements and Commitments Abroad of the Senate Committee on Foreign Relations, 91st Cong., 1st sess., part 2 (Washington: Government Printing Office, 1970).

his advisers, "even if we have to fight — with our allies or without them." [2] The President sought to justify his firm stand by two facts: (1) a request for aid from a legally constituted government and (2) the SEATO Treaty, which committed the United States to contribute to the security of the area. At that time SEATO was applicable to Laos as a protocol state, although the Lao government later repudiated this offer of protection.

President Kennedy took a quite different tack. When he met the Soviet Union's Nikita Khrushchev in Vienna in June, 1961, one of the few things on which they agreed was that Laos should be an independent and neutral country. After a year of negotiations a pact was signed at Geneva. The central idea behind it was that Laos would maintain its neutrality and that the powers would respect it. The government of Laos issued a statement of neutrality declaring that it "will not . . . recognize the protection of any alliance or military coalition, including SEATO." The United States accepted that declaration as a part of the agreement at Geneva, thus ending any obligation it might otherwise have had to go to the defense of Laos.

But neutrality for Laos proved to be elusive. While agreeing with the powers to keep out of international quarrels, the factions within Laos had agreed among themselves to set up a tripartite government made up of rightists, neutralists, and the communistic Pathet Lao. The portfolios in that government were distributed among the three factions under a formula that seemed to guarantee chaos. At that time the United States had 666 so-called military advisers in Laos, but they all withdrew under the terms of the 1962 accords. North Vietnam is thought to have had about 10,000 troops stationed in Laos at the time of the agreement, and some 6000 remained in flagrant violation of its terms. It is this double-

---

[2] Dwight D. Eisenhower, *Waging Peace 1956–1961* (New York: Doubleday, 1965), p. 610.

cross on the part of the North Vietnamese that accounts in large part for the subsequent American involvement.

Washington had ample cause for resentment over the duplicity of Hanoi. Not only did the North Vietnamese troops remain in Laos; in 1963 they joined forces with the Pathet Lao and attempted to crush the neutralists. After that experience the Royal Laotian Government called for help, and the United States supplied the military equipment requested. The next step came when the North Vietnamese stepped up their military operations in Laos and greatly increased their use of the Ho Chi Minh Trail through Laos to get troops and supplies into South Vietnam. In these circumstances the supposedly neutral Lao government agreed to more intensive training of its troops, logistics support, and American air operations over the country. In May, 1964, the Communists took over the entire Plain of Jars in Northern Laos. The Royal Government then agreed to photo reconnaissance flights and search and rescue operations over Laos from bases in Thailand. A month later armed escorts for these missions were added. Early in 1965 the United States began bombing Lao territory along the Ho Chi Minh Trail.

All this came about without any obligation on our part or real commitment to Laos. The President was disturbed about what the North Vietnamese were doing to their neighbors and evolved a policy to help the Lao maintain their independence. Through four administrations, two Republican and two Democratic, the policy evolved from one of military aid to the government to active participation in the war. But the President did not go to Congress for authority; he didn't even tell the American people what he was doing. He just took it for granted that the President, as Commander in Chief of the Armed Forces, has ample authority to carry out a foreign policy of his own making regardless of the fact that it takes the lives of American citizens.

In the hearings of the Senate Subcommittee on United

States Security Agreements and Commitments Abroad, Senator Fulbright and others sought to determine the purpose of our Lao policy. The following exchange with William H. Sullivan, Deputy Assistant Secretary of State for East Asian and Pacific Affairs, is enlightening:

SENATOR FULBRIGHT. What is the justification for continuing these activities which now become very substantial? If it is the Truman Doctrine, it seems to me something different from the United Nations. The Truman Doctrine is bilateral. It is a statement by the United States which you seem to be reiterating if I understand you correctly. At this stage, I am not trying to criticize you, but trying to understand what is the rationale of our Government for putting a very large effort into this area in Laos. Is it because we feel a unilateral obligation to maintain the independence of Laos?

MR. SULLIVAN. I do not think so, sir, and I do not think the Truman Doctrine per se has been prescribed in or prescribed for our policy in Laos.

SENATOR FULBRIGHT. If it is not the Truman Doctrine, then there is no — I do not want to quibble about what SEATO or the 1962 agreement is. I am talking now of what is the real interest of this country. Let us assume that this country is not just engaged in theories but really interested in our own defense and the national interests of the United States, if it is possible to disentangle that at least for the purpose of discussion, from any obligation under the 1962 agreement.

MR. SULLIVAN. I think I see your point.

I do not believe we have any legal obligation nor do we have any commitment that requires us to, as a nation, to insist that the independence of Laos must be preserved.

SENATOR FULBRIGHT. That is just what I mean. I am trying to clarify it.

MR. SULLIVAN. There is nothing in any documents that we have signed or in any commitments that we have undertaken that requires that. So that the policy of the United States over the past several years and currently with respect to preserving the independence or seeing that the independence or helping to see that the independence of Laos is preserved is a policy decision made by the various political leaders of the country.[3]

Senator Fulbright then wanted to know what particular interest, in the absence of any commitment, had guided the Presidents in their decisions. Was it an industrial interest, an economic interest, a political interest, or a military security interest? To this Mr. Sullivan replied: "Well, sir, I think I would describe it in fairly broad terms as a policy which has generally formed our attitude toward the prospects of stability and security in East Asia over the past postwar years, post-World War II, the assumption that the prospect for the area becoming stabilized is best assumed by the national independence of the states on the periphery of China . . ." [4] But Mr. Sullivan denied that the United States was trying to protect Laos from China. In reply to another question as to whether the military security of the United States was involved, he said: "I think there is some element of concern for the security of those forces of ours which are deployed in Vietnam." In other words, the administration seemed to be asserting a right to make war in Laos to support the presidential war in Vietnam, a doctrine that was to be asserted in bolder and more flagrant terms in connection with the 1970 invasion of the Communist sanctuaries in Cambodia.

Fulbright's summary at this point highlights the inconsistencies of the policy:

It seems to me a very anomalous situation. We pretend it [Laos] is a sovereign and independent country. We say we want to keep it sovereign and independent, but without any

[3] "United States Security Agreements and Commitments Abroad: Laos," pp. 392–393.
[4] Ibid., p. 393.

treaty or authorization I can think of, as you have already stated. But we do intervene in a major way, supply them with bombers, bombing people on their territory, and responding to General Vang Pao's request, and so on, as if we had a full-fledged treaty, very much as if he were a member of NATO.[5]

The Senate subcommittee turned a high-powered spot-light on the 1962 Geneva Accords in an effort to find some authority for what the administration was doing in Laos. Mr. Sullivan acknowledged that the accords define our basic obligations regarding Laos, but these accords are not a treaty. They committed the President to respect the neutrality of Laos and to consult with other parties to the agreements if a violation should occur or be threatened. But they set up no obligation on the part of our government to guarantee Lao neutrality against other states. And since this very document put an end to any SEATO obligation to Laos, the United States operations in that country were left dangling on the very flimsy thread of inherent executive power. Once more the record of the subcommittee hearings is instructive.

MR. PAUL [Roland A. Paul, subcommittee counsel]. In the light of that explanation with regard to SEATO, under what authority are we acting, lay SEATO aside as it applies to Laos, but under what authority are the American personnel in Laos there?

MR. SULLIVAN. They are there under the executive authority of the President.

MR. PAUL. Would you elaborate that just a little more. They are engaged in bombing and targeting bombs, and there are military advisers to the Laotian Government. What executive authority of the President are you referring to?

MR. SULLIVAN. I am not a constitutional lawyer and might come off badly on this, but the authority of the President to conduct foreign relations.

[5] Ibid., p. 400.

SENATOR SYMINGTON. Mr. Secretary, are you saying that the President of the United States, under our Constitution, can supply military spotters over a period for bombing a foreign country with which there has been no request from this Government for declaring war; that he also has the right to put U.S. military troops in airplanes over a foreign country over a period and direct the bombing of that country; that he has that right under the Constitution?

MR. SULLIVAN. I think that the President, several Presidents, throughout the history of the country have taken acts of this type on the presumption that it is within their own authority; yes, sir.

SENATOR SYMINGTON. Leaving aside the President before this President, have they done that over a period of years without the knowledge of the Congress or the American people?

MR. SULLIVAN. They have done it over a period of years, yes, sir; without specific legislative assent.

SENATOR SYMINGTON. Could you give us a couple or more illustrations of when it was done?

MR. SULLIVAN. Well, I read a very interesting compilation that ran several pages that was introduced in the floor debate by the late Senator Dirksen, and that is in the Congressional Record.

SENATOR SYMINGTON. What were two of those that impressed you the most where the President of the United States operated with American troops in a country over a period of years without referring it to the Congress in any way?

MR. SULLIVAN. Well, the Barbary Pirates is one that comes to mind back in the days of the Bey of Tunis. But there were operations throughout Latin America in the earlier part of this century.

SENATOR SYMINGTON. And the Congress knew nothing of this operation of the Barbary Pirates?

MR. SULLIVAN. Well, the Congress knew nothing, I am not sure what the Congress knew, but there was no legislative assent.[6]

---

[6] Ibid., pp. 433–434.

Members of the committee staff challenged this inaccurate statement, and later put the facts in the record. The deputy assistant secretary of state acknowledged his error, but offered no apologies and no correct statement of the facts. Actually President Thomas Jefferson had been so scrupulous about respecting the war power of Congress that he did not permit naval vessels sent out to protect American commerce against the Barbary Pirates to engage in any reprisals or offensive action. When the American defenders captured a pirate ship after a battle, the President ordered it released along with its surviving crew because he had no authority to engage in war. He then went to Congress, however, and asked for authority to smite the pirates operating from Tripoli and other North African states, and Congress readily assented. It is impossible to avoid the conclusion that an incident showing admirable respect on the part of Jefferson for the war powers of Congress was grossly distorted — thrown completely into reverse — by a high official of the State Department to buttress his argument that the President has authority to make war.

Since no legal commitments to Laos could be found anywhere, Senator Symington and his colleagues wanted to know how the decision to participate in the war in Laos was taken. Here is a sample of the response they got:

SENATOR SYMINGTON. How did you arrive at an agreement to put American pilots in American planes to target Laotian bombing of Laotian people?

MR. SULLIVAN. The decision to do this was taken here in the United States by the U.S. Government.

SENATOR SYMINGTON. Was that taken without an agreement with Souvanna Phouma?

MR. SULLIVAN. No, sir. There was a request by the Prime Minister for assistance, and the form in which it was rendered, however, was a unilateral decision by the United States.

SENATOR SYMINGTON. Then the United States agreed with what Souvanna Phouma requested; did they not?

MR. SULLIVAN. The United States undertook to respond in its own way and can change it. There is no undertaking —

SENATOR SYMINGTON. Don't let's get into a square dance about it, a semantic square dance. Souvanna Phouma requested assistance and the United States agreed to give him that kind of assistance . . .[7]

As this hassle ran on to some length, it developed that Souvanna Phouma came to the United States many times with numerous requests. While specific promises were seldom made, he got many of the things he asked for despite the absence of any specific written agreements.

The nature of the American involvement in Laos was further clarified by a description of the mysterious Project 404. In military jargon, Project 404 was approved by the Department of Defense in 1966 "to provide augmentees and logistic support for the Army and Air attachés to Laos." Originally 117 military men and five civilians were in the project. By way of camouflaging the operation, these people were assigned to the Deputy Chief, JUSMAG, Thailand, but their duty stations were in Laos. One of their foremost tasks was to coordinate the air operations of the Royal Lao Air Force and the United States air units operating over that country. Senator Symington sought to untangle the testimony of Colonel Robert L. F. Tyrrell, USAF, U.S. Air Attaché, Vientiane:

SENATOR SYMINGTON. Let me see if I understand.

Say the Ambassador decides a strike is to be made at a certain place in Laos. He gives those instructions to you and you, in turn, through project 404, give those instructions to the people

[7] Ibid., p. 437.

in Thailand and/or Vietnam, including the Fleet at Yankee Station. They will execute the strike; correct?

COLONEL TYRRELL. Essentially that is correct. Normally, if an operation in the field requires support, the request is made, and this is coordinated with all concerned, and if the Ambassador approves the requirement then we do go in with an official request for the support required.

SENATOR SYMINGTON. I understand, it can work both ways.

MR. SULLIVAN. Could I comment on that, Mr. Senator?

SENATOR SYMINGTON. Sure.

MR. SULLIVAN. Because I think there is some misunderstanding.

SENATOR SYMINGTON. Yes.

MR. SULLIVAN. Particularly the phrase that the Ambassador decides a strike should be made, and then instructions are given through Colonel Tyrrell. This is not the Ambassador's role. The Ambassador approves or disapproves whether a strike can be made, but the direction to make a strike comes from the U.S. military, 7th Air Force, or if it needs to go higher, CINCPAC. In other words, a proposal is made to Colonel Tyrrell.

SENATOR SYMINGTON. By whom?

MR. SULLIVAN. Either by the Royal Lao Air Force or by a general of the Royal Lao Army or through various intelligence antenna [deleted] which bring the suggestion to him that a strike be made.

He and his staff take a look at it, and then bring it to me or to one of my representatives. We apply, in effect, political criteria. Are there people, villagers, are there areas . . . the Prime Minister or someone has indicated should not be involved; is there a risk, for example, of being too close to China or is there anything which, in my judgment or my representative's judgment, goes beyond what is prudent to do and, if so, it is disapproved. If not, it is approved.

But then what he makes is a request to higher military authority, and higher military authority decides whether or not it will execute.[8]

[8] Ibid., pp. 458–459.

So an American airman and an American Ambassador in Vientiane were sitting in judgment on the bombing to be done in the kingdom of Laos. Colonel Tyrrell explained that he would listen to American advisers in the regions and to Lao in the regions before deciding whether a strike should be made. In some areas not accessible to the Lao the United States forces carried out target planning without consulting the Laotian military commanders. After the United States stopped bombing North Vietnam, the bombing in Laos was greatly accelerated, not in the area of the Ho Chi Minh Trail but in Northern Laos. Colonel Tyrrell sought to explain this by saying that the North Vietnamese had intensified their offensive in Laos during the rainy season, but he also acknowledged that it was due in part to the fact that more aircraft were available. Bombing in Laos was greatly increased after the bombing in North Vietnam was stopped, presumably because the American pilots didn't have anything else to do. Some sources placed the number of sorties between 12,500 and 15,000 a month, coming from American bases in Thailand against Communist areas in northern Laos as well as the Ho Chi Minh Trail.

Targets in Laos were customarily selected by the 7th Air Force in Saigon or the 7/13 Air Force located in Thailand from photographs taken by reconnaissance aircraft. When validated by the ambassador, they would go onto a list of targets to be smashed at the first opportunity. In the case of moving targets, such as trucks, boats, or enemy troops, however, they could be validated for immediate strikes by forward air guides on the ground or by Lao observers in the back seat of a United States Air Force plane.

The following note supplied for the Symington subcommittee's record by "the administration" indicates that the plane losses suffered by the United States in Laos were certainly not negligible:

In the period 1964 to Sept. 28, 1969, U.S. aircraft losses in northern Laos, including both combat and operational losses, have totalled less than 80, and U.S. aircraft losses in southern Laos somewhat less than 300. Primarily along the trail. These figures are approximate since the basis upon which earlier computations were made cannot be vouched for by this administration.[9]

By comparison with the affair in Vietnam, the flirtation with Laos is a very modest affair. The figures supplied to the Symington subcommittee showed 59 State Department employees in Laos, 15 Marine guards, 338 employees accredited to the Agency for International Development, 19 in the U.S. Information Service, and 127 assigned to the military attaché, a total of 558 hired directly. In addition, the contract personnel having some relationship to the war was listed as follows: international voluntary service 53, Air America 207, Continental Air Services 73, a total of 333. The military personnel in Laos was reported as numbering 218, but Deputy Assistant Secretary Sullivan acknowledged that "every American official in the country [Laos] is engaged in a composite effort, and one element of that effort which looms very large is military." [10] When the President made his report on Laos on March 6, 1970, the total number of Americans working in the Laotian cause, civilian and military, had increased slightly to 1040.

The government is still not willing to let the country know precisely what the venture in Laos has cost. Various witnesses at the Symington subcommittee hearings indicated that they did not have the precise figures. They were asked to submit a statement for the record, which came out as follows in the published text:

[9] Ibid., p. 380.
[10] "United States Security Agreements and Commitments Abroad: Laos," p. 506.

The total cost of all U.S. activities in Laos, including air operations against the Ho Chi Minh trail is about [deleted] billion a year. Of this, approximately [deleted] billion is related directly to our efforts in South Vietnam.[11]

Later Colonel Peter T. Russell, Deputy Chief of the Joint U.S. Military Advisory Group, disguised as operating in Thailand, said a little over $90 million was spent for military assistance of Laos during fiscal 1969. Committee members asked why a billion dollars had been allowed to go down the drain in Laos. Whatever the official cost figure is, suspicions remain that it is not complete because of the great amount of aid to Laos that was channeled through Thailand. For example, the Thai seemed to be providing Laos with airplanes, but officials later confessed that the United States replaced those planes in the Thai inventory.

It is interesting to note in passing that the United States provides about 75 per cent of the Lao military budget. The revenue collected by the Lao government is roughly equal to what it spends for nonmilitary purposes. If it is going to maintain a military establishment without cutting drastically into civilian needs, it must get about 50 per cent of its revenue from the outside, and of this portion 75 per cent is supplied by the United States and the other 25 per cent by the United Kingdom, Japan, Australia, and France. One of the ironies of the situation is that Laos, a poor country with a gross national product of only about $150 million, has become heavily dependent on this aid — aid given in defense of her neutrality and independence.

The Symington subcommittee gave a good deal more attention to the billion dollars said to have gone down the drain in Laos than it did to the casualties. The testimony of Brigadier General Donald Blackburn on casualties was de-

[11] Ibid., p. 511.

leted from the printed hearings, but the administration subsequently provided this statement:

> A careful review of the records has forced the Administration to conclude that it is not possible to provide precise figures with full confidence, because of the way casualties were tabulated and criteria applied over the various periods involved prior to the tabulating system for which this Administration is responsible. The most that can be said with confidence is that in the period 1962–69 something under 200 U.S. military personnel were killed in Laos and approximately another 200 can be listed either as missing in action or prisoners of war, but which status should be applied is unknown. Of those killed in Laos up to October 22, 1969, something around one-quarter were killed with respect to operations in northern Laos.[12]

The secrecy of the Laotian venture drew even more criticism than the cost in lives and money and the abuse of presidential powers. The official explanation for operating in the dark was that any open acknowledgment of aid to Laos would have brought Washington under condemnation from world opinion for violation of the Geneva Accords. Some diplomats also feared that candor would make it more difficult to negotiate with Moscow and thus frustrate hope of getting Lao neutrality back on the track. Actually, however, the Russians were well aware of both the North Vietnamese and American violations of the Geneva Accords, and only the American people were kept in the dark, so far as official information was concerned.

The damage that might have been done by candid statements in Washington about the evolution of chaos in Laos has been greatly exaggerated. The gross violations of the Geneva Accords by the North Vietnamese has given other parties to the agreement ample reason to take countermeas-

[12] Ibid., p. 380.

ures. Not only had Hanoi kept its troops in Laos in flagrant defiance of the accords; it had also fought the legitimate Lao government set up in accord with the Geneva settlement and had in effect appropriated a part of Laos (the Ho Chi Minh Trail) in order to facilitate its aggression against South Vietnam. The elementary principle of self-defense gave Laos ample justification in international law to seek aid against these encroachments, and the United States could scarcely be condemned under international law for responding to the call.

It is from the domestic, and not the international, viewpoint that the operation is highly vulnerable. The first thought of the President in regard to the evolving situation in Laos should have been, not what was permissible under the Geneva Accords, which after all were not treaties, but what could be legitimately done under the Constitution. He should have been thinking less about the reaction of the Russians and more about the reaction in Congress and the country. By responding impulsively to the challenge of the North Vietnamese and the appeals of Souvanna Phouma, he humiliated a great democratic power by committing it to a form of secret guerrilla warfare in imitation of communistic tactics. President Nixon sought to excuse this automatic reflex of his predecessor and himself in his statement of March 6, 1970. "The level of our air operations," he said, "has been increased only as the number of North Vietnamese in Laos and the level of their aggression has [sic] increased." [13] But only a global policeman complex would seem to require a secret, automatic response to such a challenge in remote Southeast Asia.

One reason for the secrecy becomes fully apparent from the story of Phou Pha Thi. That name is applied to a 5860-foot-high mountain in an isolated section of northern Laos near

[13] White House release, March 6, 1970, p. 5.

the border of North Vietnam — an area that was clearly in
Communist territory under the tripartite arrangement recognized in the Geneva Accords. In 1964 the United States
began, nevertheless, to build a base there for a variety of uses
in the war against North Vietnam. As Deputy Assistant
Secretary of State Sullivan later testified, "the Air Force was
particularly anxious to have this [installation] here because
it was 17 miles from the North Vietnam border and provided
excellent coverage over the entire target area. That is the
reason for the selection of this site." [14]

At first the equipment installed at Phou Pha Thi was not
manned, but by 1966 the place had become a vital complex
of radar and electronic equipment used to guide American
planes to their bombing targets in North Vietnam in bad
weather and at night. A landing strip had been built in a
narrow adjacent valley. Chartered planes flew personnel,
supplies, electronic equipment, and arms into this secret
stronghold. It is also reported to have served as a base for
"Jolly Green Giant" helicopters used to save American pilots
shot down by anti-aircraft weapons in North Vietnam and for
American-led teams of Meo warriors engaged in harassment
operations.[15] The place was supposed to be impregnable because of the precipitous mountain walls on three sides and a
formidable array of Meo soldiers and American weapons on
the fourth.

All the factors that made this "radar facility" valuable to
the United States military combined to make it intolerable
to Hanoi. North Vietnam launched several assaults against
it and finally overwhelmed the defenders on March 11, 1968.
The last battle is reported to have taken place in a grotto
where twelve Americans, a number of Laotian officers, and

[14] "United States Security Agreements and Commitments Abroad: Laos," p. 490.
[15] See T. D. Allman's dispatch in the *Washington Post*, March 16, 1970, p. 1.

possibly 100 Meo soldiers were killed. The Johnson administration made no report on this hidden disaster to the American people. By way of concealing the venture the casualties were listed as having occurred in "Southeast Asia." [16] Two years after the incident President Nixon was still trying to hide it. In his March 6, 1970, statement he said: "No American stationed in Laos has ever been killed in ground combat operations." [17] His sweeping assertion also ignored some other casualties that were later acknowledged, but the continued pretense that nothing happened at Phou Pha Thi seemed to set a new watermark in deception to protect the White House from public indignation over presidential warmaking. In the same speech the President said of the aid given to Laos: "It is limited. It is requested. It is supportive and defensive . . . It has been necessary to protect American lives in Vietnam and to preserve a precarious but important balance in Laos." The operation at Phou Pha Thi could be more accurately described as provocative, reckless, and in conflict with the supposed aim of neutrality for Laos.

The Symington subcommittee report itself stopped far short of fully disclosing the Laos affair. The published version is riddled with deletions. Apparently the largest gap results from the elimination of all the testimony concerning the participation of the Central Intelligence Agency in the operations in Laos. CIA Director Richard Helms testified in the hearings, but what he said did not survive the administration's censorship. From many other sources, however, the story of the CIA's involvement is known, at least in part. A series of articles by Henry Kamm in the *New York Times* in October, 1969, disclosed that the CIA was training and supplying a clandestine army of Meo tribesmen in

[16] "United States Security Agreements and Commitments Abroad: Laos," p. 849.
[17] White House press release of March 6, 1970, p. 5.

northern Laos under the command of General Vang Pao. The strength of General Pao's guerrilla forces was estimated at 40,000, and they were deemed to be the most effective fighting unit in Laos. The CIA was said to provide this Armée Clandestine with intelligence, communications, logistics, and other aid.[18] Additional details were supplied by various other writers.[19]

Some members of Congress knew about the operation from State Department and Pentagon briefings and from their travels in Southeast Asia. Nevertheless, the details remained highly classified. The fullest official disclosure came in October, 1969, from an interview that Senator Fulbright gave to the news media after the CIA director had testified before the investigating subcommittee of which Fulbright is a member.[20] Fulbright estimated the strength of the Meo Army under General Vang Pao at 36,000. He said that it is engaged in a "regular civil war"; that it was a "major operation" with costs running "in the neighborhood of $150 to $160 million in 1969"; that "we supply all of the arms, and training, the ammunition, the transportation from one area to another"; that the Armée Clandestine was backed up by an enormous air force, helicopters and military planes, operating out of Thailand; and that the CIA was acting under orders from the National Security Council and a committee appointed by the council, which is directly responsible to the President.

Responding to Fulbright's disclosures, which proved to be front-page news, Secretary of State Rogers talked as if the information given were common knowledge, even though the State Department had kept it highly classified. "I had

[18] See the *New York Times,* October 28, 1969, and February 5, 1970.
[19] See Jack Foisie's story in the *Washington Post,* November 2, 1969, p. A24; also Peter R. Kann's dispatch to the *Wall Street Journal,* December 18, 1969, p. 1.
[20] *Washington Post,* October 29, 1969, p. 1.

thought that the Congress was familiar with the developments in Laos," he said.[21]

"This is really quite extraordinary," Fulbright retorted. "It is quite ordinary for a dictatorship, but [for us] to be conducting . . . as large a war as this without authorization is quite unusual."

Senator Symington later commented on the same set of circumstances in these words:

> We incur hundreds of thousands of U.S. casualties because we are opposed to a closed society. We say we are an open society, and the enemy is a closed society. Accepting that premise, it would appear logical for them not to tell their people [what they were doing]; but it is a sort of a twist on our basic philosophy about the importance of containing communism.
>
> Here we are telling Americans they must fight and die to maintain an open society, but not telling our people what we are doing. That would seem the characteristic of a closed society.[22]

The secrecy of the operation aroused another storm when John A. Hannah, Administrator of the Agency for International Development, acknowledged that AID provided a cover for anti-Communist operations in Laos. AID had more than 230 Americans on its payroll in Laos, many of them under disguise as "community development advisers," "air traffic control advisers," engineers, or "area coordinators." Although Hannah insisted that Laos was the only place in the world where CIA agents had been allowed to masquerade as employees of an AID mission, that practice, initiated in 1962 and followed by three administrations, added sub-

[21] *Washington Post,* October 30, 1969, p. 1.
[22] "United States Security Agreements and Commitments Abroad: Laos," p. 543.

stantially to the incredibility gap that has been afflicting American foreign relations. Another aspect of the problem also troubled many citizens at home: the insidious longevity of evil practices through both Democratic and Republican administrations when they are concealed from public view.

Fear that hidden American participation in the war in Laos might burgeon into another large-scale conflict induced Congress to erect a barrier to such further involvement in December, 1969. A Senate amendment to the defense appropriations bill forbidding use of any of the funds "to finance the introduction of American ground combat troops into Laos or Thailand" was accepted also by the House and finally approved by the President. The same bill placed a $2.5 billion limit on aid to the same two countries. It was the first time that Congress had directly intervened to curb the discretion of the President in directing the war in Southeast Asia.

As this fantastic hidden war was finally dragged out into the daylight, millions of Americans asked themselves if there was no limit to the President's role as policeman to the world. Here is a storybook country on the other side of the globe of which we have very little understanding. By common consent of all the interested powers it repudiated the safeguards that SEATO had sought to throw about it and deliberately chose the hazards of neutralism. Washington was as pleased with this policy as any of the other powers at the time because the course Laos takes is not vital to our security. Yet when the little kingdom was victimized by one of its neighbors, President Johnson took it upon himself to authorize an underground war of his own, which, however worthy his motive, could have sparked (or could yet spark) a holocaust.

However one looks at it, this is globalism running riot. It is wholly beside the point that the Presidents who initiated it and carried it forward want peace. So did the Caesars, Napoleon, and the modern dictators. They all wanted peace on their own terms. Undoubtedly the President's terms are more just and humane and more in line with the basic human yearning for freedom. Nevertheless, the fact remains that a war carried on by the President for what he deems a worthy cause, without the knowledge of the country and without the consent of Congress, is a negation of the democratic process that he claims to be defending. It is also a negation of the principle of collective defense on which the fate of the free world seems to hinge in these perilous times.

Relatively small though it is, therefore, the war in Laos is a shocking symbol of what is wrong with American foreign policy in the postwar era. We have allowed our Presidents to tangle with an assortment of little tyrants in their kind of lethal games, with virtually no accountability to the people between the quadrennial elections. It is not only globalism running riot; it is also personalized, hidden, and irresponsible government running riot. Unless it is brought under control, it could lead to the destruction of our democratic system, with disastrous consequences for the causes of both peace and freedom.

V

Our Entanglement with Thailand

THE TENDENCY of a loose alliance to evolve into an entangling commitment is well illustrated by our relations with Thailand. As early as 1950 the United States entered into agreements pledging economic and technical aid and mutual defense assistance to the Thai. Four years later the two countries joined with six others in adhering to the SEATO Treaty, which pledged each to act in accord with its constitutional processes to meet any armed attack against a member state. With substantial help from the United States, the Thai increased their security expenditures by 250 per cent between 1954 and 1959.

The ancient kingdom of Thailand was deemed to be in special danger because of the progress the Communists were making in their efforts to take over neighboring Laos. In the summer of 1960 the King of Thailand visited Washington and secured from President Eisenhower a reaffirmation of "unwavering determination" on the part of the United States "fully to honor its treaty commitments undertaken in the cause of collective security." After the inauguration of President Kennedy, he gave the Thai similar reassurance and made what the State Department called "small deployments . . . to meet special situations."[1] Then followed the agree-

[1] "United States Security Agreements and Commitments Abroad: Kingdom

ment between Secretary of State Dean Rusk and Thailand's Foreign Minister, Thanat Khomen, which put a new face on this partnership reaching halfway around the globe.

In effect the Rusk-Thanat agreement grafted onto the SEATO Treaty a bilateral arrangement for putting down Communist aggression. They first recognized that "the Treaty provides the basis for the signatories collectively to assist Thailand in case of Communist armed attack against that country." Secretary Rusk gave assurance that the United States would give "full effect" to this obligation it had undertaken whether or not the other parties to the treaty joined in defense of Thailand. The generalities of SEATO were thus superseded by the specifics of Rusk-Thanat. Along with this transformation of the partnership went pledges of more American aid and a promise of "effective cooperation in social, economic and military measures" through the Joint Thai–United States Committee that had been previously established.[2]

Although the State Department insisted that the nature of the SEATO Treaty had not in any way been altered, the more intimate nature of this bilateral understanding soon became apparent. The spring of 1962 brought new advances for the Communist forces in Laos and thus accentuated the worries of the Thai. By way of demonstrating the United States' intentions President Kennedy set up a Military Assistance Command for Thailand (MACTHAI) and sent about 10,000 American ground and Air Force personnel to the jittery land of Siam. In part the operation was connected with a SEATO military exercise, but the President also acknowledged that his action was taken in order to put the United States in a position to fulfill our obligations under

of Thailand," hearings before the Subcommittee on United States Security Agreements and Commitments Abroad, of the Senate Committee on Foreign Relations, 91st. Cong., 1st. sess., part 3 (Washington: Government Printing Office, 1970), p. 614.

[2] State Department press release No. 145, March 6, 1962.

the Manila Pact (SEATO) and "to help insure the territorial integrity of Thailand."[3] The troops were withdrawn between July and December, 1962.

It seems impossible to escape the conclusion that President Kennedy had decided to defend Thailand against a Communist attack, with American manpower, if such an attack should materialize. The SEATO Treaty had pledged that each country would respond to a Communist threat in the area through its constitutional processes, which had been officially interpreted as meaning with the approval of Congress, but JFK acted solely on his own responsibility. In one other respect he interpreted the treaty in a way that was never intended by its authors. Secretary Dulles, the chief architect of the SEATO alliance, told the Senate in its hearings on consent to ratification of the treaty:

> We do not intend to dedicate any major elements of the U.S. Military Establishment to form an army in defense of this area. We rely primarily upon the deterrence of our mobile striking power. That we made clear to our associates in the Treaty and that is our policy. It would involve, in the opinion of our military advisers, an injudicious over extension of our military power if we were to try to build up that kind of an organization in Southeast Asia. We do not have adequate forces to do it, and I believe that should there be an open armed attack in that area, the most effective step would be to strike at the source of aggression rather than to try to rush American manpower in the area to try to fight a ground war. So that we do not intend, Mr. Chairman, to have under this treaty any such local combined forces as have been created in Europe under the North Atlantic Treaty . . .[4]

Senator H. Alexander Smith, who had been a delegate to the SEATO Conference, also gave the Senate, in the course

[3] "United States Security Agreements and Commitments Abroad: Thailand," p. 615.
[4] Ibid., pp. 692–693.

of the debate on ratification, assurance that the treaty involved no compulsory arrangement for American military participation in case of an attack and no commitment of American ground forces to the Asian mainland. "We carefully avoided," he said, "any possible implication of that kind." [5] Despite these precautions taken in the creation of SEATO, the avoidance of American involvement in a land war in Thailand in 1962 appears to have been more a matter of good luck or of Communist weakness than of adherence to the original intent of the treaty.

Under another agreement concluded in 1963 the United States supplied Thailand with locomotives and rolling stock designed to support possible emergency operations of SEATO forces. The same accord led to upgrading the air base at Nakhon Phanom and to the "prepositioning" of such items as ordnance, engineer equipment, and so forth. In mid-1964, with the outlook in Laos and South Vietnam still deteriorating, American and Thai authorities began to work out a military contingency plan that could be put into effect with the approval of both governments should an emergency arise.

Probably too much furor has been raised over this contingency plan. It aroused deep suspicion in the Senate, when reports of its existence finally leaked out, because the Pentagon had labeled it top-secret and officials refused to talk about it. Senator Fulbright and others feared that it contained far-reaching commitments by the United States that had never been submitted to the Senate for its advice and consent. The State Department insisted that it was not really an intergovernmental agreement but only a military blueprint setting forth what the two governments would probably do under the pressure of an emergency if both should agree at the time. Fulbright pressed his case against the contingency plan at the Symington subcommittee hear-

[5] Ibid.

ings on United States security agreements and commitments abroad, asserting that an agreement reaching beyond the terms of the SEATO Treaty had been made and that no one would ever have heard of it, except by chance. The following exchange throws some light on the controversy:

AMBASSADOR [LEONARD] UNGER [United States Ambassador to Thailand]. Senator, my understanding of our situation with Thailand in this field is that there is no commitment except for the SEATO Treaty which was approved by the U.S. Senate. There is no other security arrangement of that nature.

SENATOR FULBRIGHT. That is a theory, but it came out in evidence the other day that we are doing in Thailand a great many of the things already which were provided for in the contingency planning, and which are certainly not provided for in SEATO.

AMBASSADOR UNGER. Senator, it seems to me that it would be important to make a distinction between what we have committed ourselves to do in the sense of using American forces, in a sense of going to war, taking military action on the one hand and, on the other hand, being prepared so that if there does develop the kind of a situation in which we should decide that we do want to act, we and our allies would be able to act. In other words, the availability of —

SENATOR FULBRIGHT. What bothers me is you can act without the Congress ever knowing anything about it, or the public knowing anything about it. Actually, it is the procedure that I am questioning. You can and you have done nearly everything outlined in the Thai Contingency Plan except provide ground troops.

AMBASSADOR UNGER. . . . we would not be in any position to act under our SEATO commitment except as I received from Washington an official instruction to proceed. In other words, I would regard that as absolutely essential to any action that was taken.[6]

[6] Ibid., p. 656.

Whether or not the contingency plan added anything to the SEATO commitment depends, of course, on how one looked at it. Thai Prime Minister Thanom described it in 1970 as "putting in practice cooperation between Thailand and the United States to help prevent Communist aggression." He went on to say that the plan "gives us the certainty and confidence that the United States will not desert us and let us fight against the Communists on our own." [7] Although Thai officials agreed that the plan was not automatically binding, because action under it would have to be approved by both governments, they had reason to suppose that the United States would respond as it had done in 1962, if the situation seemed to warrant direct American intervention.

This is precisely what senatorial critics of the contingency plan were afraid of. They knew, of course, that Thailand could not possibly put a joint defense arrangement into effect, acting alone. The United States would have to give its consent, but the Kennedy precedent in Thailand and the Johnson precedent in Vietnam created a presumption that the President would take full responsibility for any U.S. participation in a Thai crisis, without seeking authority from Congress as was required by the SEATO reference to "constitutional processes." As recently as August, 1969, a spokesman for the State Department, Robert J. McCloskey, indicated that implementation of the contingency plan would need executive action only.[8] The furor that was raised in Congress was designed to upset this understanding and give Congress an opportunity to assess any crisis before American troops could be committed to another land war in Asia.

In some degree this appears to have been accomplished. In the heat of the controversy both President Nixon and Secretary of State Rogers insisted that the contingency plan

[7] Ibid., p. 880.
[8] *New York Times,* August 16, 1969, p. 1.

"doesn't have any binding effect." [9] Rogers undercut the McCloskey remark about executive implementation by saying that the President would consult Congress in any appropriate circumstances. Secretary of Defense Melvin R. Laird indicated that the contingency plan does not have his support and that he does not "agree with using American troops without proper consultation and advice of the Congress." [10] Although Laird stopped short of saying that he would advise the President to seek authority from Congress before using any American forces under the contingency plan, that seemed to be the implication of his remarks. Since the President did not indicate what his attitude would be, however, the contingency plan remained a source of concern among those familiar with our automatic military responses to many crises in the comparatively recent past.

The United States began its major build-up of military forces in Thailand in 1964. During March of that year six F–100s were sent to Ta Khli. After the Tonkin Gulf incident took the United States into the war in Vietnam as an active participant more men and planes were sent to Thailand. By the end of the year U.S. Air Force personnel in Thailand numbered 3000, and they had a supporting fleet of about 75 aircraft. Early in 1965 attacks on Pleiku led to the bombing of North Vietnam, with the resulting expansion of the USAF in Thailand to 9000 men and 200 aircraft. For three additional years this build-up continued. The 606th Air Commando Squadron was sent in to train the Royal Thai Air Force in counterinsurgency early in 1966. For some months this unit also provided helicopter support for Thai counterinsurgency operations, until the Thai acquired helicopters of their own.

[9] Secretary Rogers' news conference, August 20, 1969. State Department press release No. 246.
[10] Richard Homan in the *Washington Post,* August 22, 1969, p. A14.

Initially this use of American helicopters and pilots was started, not through an agreement between the two countries or by order of the President, the State Department, or the Pentagon, but by order of the American ambassador in Bangkok, Graham A. Martin. An insurgency problem developed in Thailand's historically neglected northeast section before the training program for Thai pilots had been completed and before helicopters could be delivered to the Thai under the U.S. military assistance program. Fearing that the rebels might get out of control, Martin assigned ten American helicopters to what he called "taxi service" for the Thai forces fighting the insurgents. Although the American pilots were instructed to avoid any involvement in combat operations and to ferry the Thai soldiers only to the vicinity of the fighting, not to the actual scene of combat, an American military unit became a logistical arm of the royal forces in a little civil war without the knowledge or consent of the government in Washington.

The story came to light in the Symington subcommittee hearings with Ambassador Martin as the witness:

SENATOR COOPER. I assume that your activity was initiated by direction and authority from Washington?

MR. MARTIN. No, sir. It was initiated on my own authority, and it was subsequently enlarged by the provision of enough helicopters, I think an additional 14, which made up a whole squadron. The original use of the 10, which I arranged for personally on my own authority, was done because I did not wish to repeat the mistakes which I thought had been made elsewhere, in losing the opportunity to get the Thai involvement in the containment of this insurgency set back by another dry season, which would have taken place if we had waited for the completion of the training program and the provision of the helicopters from the United States.[11]

[11] "United States Security Agreements and Commitments Abroad: Thailand," p. 903.

The incident is indicative of the casual way in which the United States has often become involved in military operations abroad in recent years. In the case of Thailand it merges into a general pattern of increasing entanglement. In the same year, 1966, three additional squadrons of F–4s and F–105s were added to the American forces stationed in Thailand for use against North Vietnam. B–52 bombers began operating against targets in North Vietnam from the Royal Thai Air Force Base of U-Tapao in 1967. By the end of that year 13 B–52s were in operation from U-Tapao, and arrangements had been made for ten more to join in the air war. The total number of American aircraft in Thailand had swelled to 527, and more than 33,000 men were there to operate them. The maximum authorized strength for American military forces in Thailand was reached in August, 1969, when about 48,000 were present.

The Thai became increasingly apprehensive over the extent of their involvement with the United States. After the bombing of North Vietnam targets from Thai bases leaked out, they expressed fear of Communist retaliation. Our forces in Thailand were also much aware of the possibility that they might be attacked from the air. These mutual fears led to the granting of additional anti-aircraft artillery to the Royal Thai Army. The United States also agreed to provide some anti-aircraft missiles and to participate in a joint air defense system, further indicating how involvement feeds upon itself.

A change in the trend did come, however, in September, 1969, when President Nixon ordered a reduction in our forces in Thailand by 6000. Thai officials had indicated that they were fed up with the widespread belief in the United States that our troops were in Thailand to defend that country, whereas in fact most of them were there in connection with the wars in Vietnam and Laos. The Thai government sought a discussion on the continued American military presence, and the reduction of forces followed.

Enormous sums were spent to support our military program in Thailand. The cost of the bases and other facilities mounted from $97 million for the years prior to 1963 to $135,800,000 for 1967 alone. After the bases were completed these outlays dropped to $24,300,000 in 1968 and then more than doubled to $54 million in 1969. The total cost of the U.S. construction program in Thailand was $702 million, which, in the words of Senator Symington, is "quite a bit of money." Congress doled out the funds with a minimum of questions. The average congressman knew little about the operation except the fact that hundreds of millions were flowing into Thailand in support of the war.

A memorandum prepared by the staff of the Symington subcommittee shows how such appropriations were handled on Capitol Hill:

On May 5, 1965, the Senate Committees on Appropriations and Armed Services held a joint hearing, H.R. 447, the Supplemental Appropriations, Department of Defense, 1965, Emergency Fund, Southeast Asia. That was held at the request of Secretary McNamara. This resolution waived the provision of the law requiring authorization hearings on legislation. Of the total $700 million requested, $107 million was requested for military construction in Southeast Asia and no detailed breakdown was provided the committee by Secretary McNamara at these hearings, nor was any provided prior to the vote which occurred the following day.

At that hearing, Secretary McNamara pointed out that, although it is not publicized because of the sensitivity of the Thai Government, the United States was utilizing Thai bases in connection with strikes against North Vietnam; moreover because of the very rapid increase in the number of strikes, the United States would be forced to continue to use these bases.

Such continued use, according to the Secretary, would necessitate the building of a pipeline from Bangkok to Korat in the center of Thailand in order to supply the petroleum dumps at the advanced airfields. A portion of the $107 million . . . would be used for this purpose . . .

The committee met in executive session following the 1 day of hearings and reported the bill to the Senate for consideration.

May 6, 1965. Based on a previous unanimous consent agreement . . . the bill was taken up and disposed of the day following the hearing.

June 4, 1965, Secretary McNamara sent a letter to the chairman outlining in greater detail how the Defense Department planned to expend $107 million requested for military construction including approximately $8,740,000 for construction in Thailand . . . the committee did not know at the time of the vote what specific bases in Thailand were included in the $107 million for construction.

According to the attached legislative history furnished by the Department of Defense, second paragraph, the committee was informed. This is true; however, they were not informed until after the fact, that is, after the vote to appropriate the funds. Later in this same session of Congress but for the next fiscal year, 1966, the Defense Department requested an additional $1,700 million for the Southeast Asia Emergency Fund. This was presented as an amendment to the fiscal 1966 defense appropriations bill, H.R. 9221, which was submitted to the House on June 17 and passed on June 23. It then passed the Senate on August 25, went to conference with final passage of the Senate on September 21, and [was] signed into law on September 29, 1965 . . . authorization was waived . . .

Prior to this Secretary McNamara was told by the committee that they wanted a shopping list of what the Department of Defense was going to use the money for. At first Secretary McNamara was reluctant to provide any such list but the staff did obtain same and had it available on the floor at the time of the debate. The Senators involved in the debate advised the Senate that said list was available, that is, from the committee. Yet according to recollection, only one Senator asked to see the list. Following these two additional requests for construction funds for Southeast Asia, including Thailand, the committee sought and was provided information prior to consideration of the legislation in question. However, it would appear that the earlier requests for funds which gave the Defense Department authority to construct bases in Thailand were voted almost blindly.[12]

In retrospect it appears that the Johnson administration also acted "almost blindly" or at least with very short-range vision. The construction of these costly bases for the bombing of North Vietnam took place largely in 1966 and 1967 and the bombing stopped in November, 1968. Construction of the great base at U-Tapao began in 1966 but the addition of facilities to accommodate B–52s was not completed until January, 1969. Of course, the bases continued to have some value in connection with our military operations in South Vietnam, but is it possible to justify the spending of more than $600 million and our deep entanglement with Thailand for this purpose?

Senator Symington asked Ambassador Unger if there was any arrangement to get anything back from what we have built in Thailand. The ambassador replied: ". . . generally speaking the answer is no, that there are no arrangements on that score . . . we have no written agreements with the Royal Thai Government regarding the ownership of the military facilities the United States has built in Thailand. There are no American bases there. We have, however, with the approval of the Royal Thai Government, improved, expanded and upgraded Thai bases and facilities." [13] The

[12] Ibid. pp. 733–734.
[13] Ibid., p. 736.

United States owns none of the land on which the bases were constructed. When it was necessary to acquire private land for this purpose, the United States bought it but deeded it over to the Thai government.

The Symington subcommittee questioned Ambassador Martin on whether there were any "secondary purposes" behind our large-scale construction program in Thailand — secondary to prosecution of the war in Vietnam. "To my infinite regret," the ambassador replied, "the answer is negative." "Why do you say to your regret?" the committee counsel asked. After some inconsequential sparring Mr. Martin responded:

> When you engage in construction of this magnitude, and again taking into experience my own background, I myself think that it was improvident and extravagant not to have given some thought to whatever military requirements might be deemed to be for American force dispositions in the decade of the seventies.
>
> Now, I am not competent to make that kind of judgment, but I felt that that kind of consideration should have gone into the decisions that were made.
>
> To the best of my knowledge and belief, they were not, and the decisions were made at the direction of the Secretary of Defense totally on the basis of their utility in the prosecution of the Vietnam war and with no other considerations allowed to be introduced at all.[14]

After taking further testimony, Senator Symington commented:

> "So when we went into Thailand, there was no effort, you have so testified, to make any kind of arrangement incident to how long we could be there or under what circumstances; in

[14] Ibid., p. 886.

fact for a long time the Thai specified that we not admit we were there at all, correct?"

"That is correct," Mr. Martin acknowledged.[15]

Considering the magnitude of the American operation in Thailand, it is pertinent to inquire what the Thai themselves were doing in regard to the Communist menace in Southeast Asia. As previously noted, most of our military spending in Thailand was for bases for use in the Vietnam war, but it is not accurate to say that this was wholly an American purpose. Washington undertook to defend South Vietnam because it was in danger of being overrun and absorbed by the Communist government in Hanoi and because the whole of Southeast Asia was deemed to be in danger of guerrilla operations, if not open aggression, from Red China. Obviously Thailand had a more direct interest in thwarting these attacks upon its immediate neighbors than did the United States, and, as a member of SEATO, it had an equal obligation to lend international aid. Thailand recognized this in a minor way, but it was not until the United States agreed to pick up most of the tab for its Vietnamese contingents that any substantial numbers were sent.

The Thai had a small air contingent in Vietnam and had arranged to add a small naval unit when the agreement for American assistance was reached in November, 1967. Under that agreement a two-brigade division of Thai volunteers called Black Panthers began operations in Vietnam early in 1969. With combat support and combat service support units, the Black Panthers had a total strength of something more than 11,000. They functioned under the operational control of U.S. II Field Force. The United States did not pay the entire cost of this Thai contribution to the conflict in

[15] Ibid., p. 888.

Vietnam. Rather, it undertook to save the Thai from any "additional financial burden" because of their contribution, which meant that we would cover all the additional costs connected with sending these troops outside of Thailand, including overseas allowances, logistic support, mustering-out pay, and so forth. U.S. allowances for Thai soldiers ranged from $39 a month for privates to $450 a month for lieutenant generals. Death and disability allowances amounted to $2500 for enlisted men and $5500 for officers. The mustering-out bonus was $400 per volunteer. In addition we agreed to reimburse the Thai for training and transporting these troops. When Thai officials complained that, with their best troops abroad, they would be less able to cope with insurgency at home, the U.S. negotiators boosted the Military Assistance Programs from $60 million to $75 million in the fiscal years 1968 and 1969 (a total of $30 million extra) so as to accelerate the modernization of the Thai forces that remained at home. Further assistance was given by providing a battery of Hawk anti-aircraft missiles for the defense of Thailand.

With this generous aid, one might expect the Thai to take over at least a proportional share of the suffering and casualties resulting from the common cause, but the information we have on that subject is not reassuring. Senator Symington tried to put the facts on record in the hearings on United States commitments abroad, with this result:

SENATOR SYMINGTON. How many casualties have they had, killed in action in Vietnam?
AMBASSADOR UNGER. I believe it is in the neighborhood of [deleted].
SENATOR SYMINGTON. [Deleted]. Our population is 200 million, and our casualties now are close to 300,000 including 39,350 dead. Would you say theirs is a comparable effort?
AMBASSADOR UNGER. Excuse me, Senator, I believe you asked for the number killed. The casualties are a good deal more.

SENATOR SYMINGTON. I beg your pardon [deleted] killed. How many wounded?

AMBASSADOR UNGER. I believe the total casualty figure is something like [deleted].

SENATOR SYMINGTON. So 33 million people with some [deleted] fighting an enemy in a country, in effect, on their border . . . Well, we say, if it is SEATO, it is a partnership, something we agreed on. So we fight. But we don't let our military fight the way they would like to fight, and have been trained to fight. Then, we take nearly all the casualties. Nobody else takes hardly any. This is what some of us just cannot understand about our policy . . .[16]

We have some 40 per cent of our army in Vietnam. We pay Thailand heavy money, but they only have some 14 per cent of their army in Vietnam.[17]

The general picture of our relations with Thailand during the 1960s is one of increasing entanglement, with very limited benefits for ourselves. The decade began with a loose defensive alliance and ended with a vast American presence in that ancient kingdom and with elaborate military plans for joint defense operations if they should become necessary. Formal commitments had perhaps remained the same, but the facts of political and military involvement had drastically changed. Although most of the American presence was directly related to the war in Vietnam, the other side of the coin is that the two countries had become partners in that venture as well as in the defense of Thailand. Such partnerships do not dissolve overnight. The building of the Thai bases at a cost of more than $600 million and the increasing merger of American and Thai interests that accompanied that operation must be regarded as an integral part of our overextension in Southeast Asia.

[16] Ibid., pp. 661–662.
[17] Ibid., p. 706.

It is sometimes said that Thailand could not become another Vietnam in the sense of being the scene of another land war for Americans on the mainland of Asia — that we have learned too much in Vietnam to make the same mistake again. But this overlooks the facts that Thailand has been an inseparable part of the Vietnam experience we have just been through and that it remains an embarrassing part of the great international dilemma confronting us as we try to extricate ourselves from the military quagmire of Asia.

The ultimate question that must be answered is whether the United States has a sufficient interest in Southeast Asia to justify the political, diplomatic, and moral commitments that have evolved out of our military operations there. We must first be clear about what it is that has lured us into our present predicament. The Symington subcommittee did a good deal of probing in this area, and the discussion always gravitated to the menace of Communist China. The following exchange is typical:

SENATOR FULBRIGHT. The whole operation, our presence there. Isn't it really inspired by our concern about Communist expansion, Chinese expansion specifically?

AMBASSADOR UNGER. Well, yes, in a sense that it is Chinese Communist expansion that is regarded by Thais and by us as what is the real threat to their independence.

SENATOR FULBRIGHT. That is the real justification.

AMBASSADOR UNGER. And we are trying to preserve, trying to help them preserve, their independence.

SENATOR FULBRIGHT. That is the real justification for our presence in Thailand.

AMBASSADOR UNGER. Well, about, I do not know, about nine-tenths of the people or more than nine-tenths of the people we have there are because of the war in Vietnam.

SENATOR FULBRIGHT. I can say the same for the war in Vietnam . . . Well now, if you can agree that this is the reason, the containment of Chinese expansionism, do you agree that it threatens Thailand as well as Vietnam?

AMBASSADOR UNGER. For Thailand I would say this is a prime factor.

SENATOR FULBRIGHT. It is the prime factor? There is no other factor, is there?

AMBASSADOR UNGER. Well, this is the threat that we are trying to help to meet.[18]

But does the vague and unmeasurable danger that China may encroach upon her neighbors justify our investment of so much flesh and blood, so much psychological anguish, and so much of our national energy and resources in an effort to stop it? Can anyone demonstrate that the independence of Thailand — or South Vietnam — is essential to our national security? It is interesting to note that the official spokesman for the State Department did not try to do so when backed into a corner by the skeptics of the Symington subcommittee. Counsel asked pointedly how the independence of Thailand relates to U.S. security. Ambassador Unger replied:

Well, Mr. Counsel, I think that the factor of Thailand's location in this particular point is not really pertinent if we are talking about a world order, the kind of thing that was envisaged in the United Nations Charter, the kind of thing that we have certainly many times spoken of, of the importance of independent countries being able to feel secure in their independence and free from the threat of an aggressor from outside, then I feel that Thailand's case is as important as any other case.

I am not saying that Thailand has the direct security meaning to us that a country much closer to us would have: but I am saying that in this context it seems to me it is an essential country, and particularly a country that is established as

[18] Ibid., pp. 859–860.

an independent country, a country that has been independent, that has shown a capacity to govern itself, to manage its own affairs responsibly in the world, even to play a role as Thailand has on a number of occasions in the international scene, such as in the Korean action in the U.N. and the present action in Vietnam.

In a circumstance like that, it seems to me, let's say, the ability of the Communists to take such a country over is a matter that would certainly seriously undermine the effort to establish some kind of a rule of law in the world.[19]

Two ideas leap out of this heavily padded verbiage: First, that the United States has inherited some kind of unilateral obligation to protect the rights of other countries envisaged in the United Nations Charter and, second, that our basic task is "to establish some kind of a rule of law in the world." Despite the guarded tone, we have here a clear proclamation of the world policeman role.

The underlying question is not, of course, whether the independence of small nations, the U.N. Charter, and the rule of law in the world are worthy objectives. Virtually all free peoples, and certainly an overwhelming majority of Americans, are committed to these ideals. The practical question that must be resolved is whether a single official, sitting in the White House with his advisers, shall be allowed to commit our nation and the lives of its citizens to the attainment of these ideals by military means — on the basis of vague alliances or our emotional attachment to the idea of world law — whenever he feels the urge to assume the policeman's role. Beyond this domestic issue is the even larger international question of the self-appointed lawgiver and law-enforcer.

However desirable it may be to save the independence of Thailand and other small countries halfway around the

[19] Ibid., pp. 644–645.

globe, it is patently absurd to pretend that their security is essential to our own. Their integrity is an international problem, not a special charge, divine or otherwise, upon the United States. Our government reacted with indignation and firmness when the Soviet Union, on the basis of its special affinity with the Castro regime, sought to establish missile bases in Cuba. No nation cared to challenge our determination to have the last word in defense of the Western Hemisphere. But we seem to expect understanding and tolerance abroad when we try to impose our brand of international law and order on remote countries in Asia and in the process build formidable military bases within close striking range of China and the Soviet Union.

Our experience with Thailand is no more a guide to sound relations with Asian countries than our experience with Vietnam. After listening for some weeks to testimony about our commitments throughout the world, Senator Symington commented one day: "We are the self-appointed baby-sitters of the world, and could be going broke doing it." [20] If the American people do not rebel against this policy, our allies and our protégés abroad probably will. It is not a sound relationship on which a stable international society can be built.

[20] Ibid., p. 756.

VI

Cambodia and the Nixon Doctrine

IN THE FIRST FIFTEEN MONTHS of the Nixon administration the United States appeared to be pulling back from its over-extended position in the world. Secretary of State Rogers had expounded his policy of the "lowered profile," meaning that the United States intended to listen more and to throw its weight around less frequently. President Nixon's plan of withdrawing American troops from Vietnam was in operation, and the so-called Nixon Doctrine outlined at Guam threw new emphasis on regional defense arrangements, with less reliance on American military might. On April 30, 1970, however, the trend seemed to be shattered by the President's announcement that he was sending American combat troops into Cambodia.

The Nixon Doctrine was not, of course, a policy of withdrawal from Asia. As restated in the President's "state of the world" report to Congress on February 18, 1970, it called rather for wider sharing of security obligations. The President pledged that the United States would stand by its treaty commitments and would "provide a shield" if any nuclear power should threaten an ally or other nation whose security was deemed vital to our own. In cases of conventional aggression, he promised to provide military and economic assistance "when requested and as appropriate." But each country seeking U.S. help would be expected "to assume the primary responsibility of providing the manpower for its defense." [1] It was a rational division of international responsibility. Although it came to be resented by countries relying too heavily on American arms, it was widely applauded by American taxpayers and by others who were apprehensive about the worsening American image abroad.

As applied to Vietnam, the Nixon Doctrine came to be known as "Vietnamization." In South Korea it was translated into plans for withdrawal of one of the two American divisions still standing guard against further aggression from the north. In Europe it stood for larger national contributions to NATO so as to relieve the excessive burden carried by the United States. Attempts to apply the doctrine in each of these cases gave rise to formidable problems, and a veritable furor arose when commentators and critics tried to appraise the invasion of the Cambodian sanctuaries by this standard.

Did the Nixon administration undermine its own bridge to a sustainable foreign policy by its impetuous use of force in this instance and by the aid it later gave to the South Vietnamese invasion of Laos? Differing opinions are almost as numerous as individual comments, and the sages who presume to speak for history have not yet rendered their verdict. An examination of the issues on both sides may, however, throw some light on problems that still lie ahead.

In his address to the nation on April 30, the President explained his opening of a new theater of combat in Indochina as an essential means of protecting American fighting men in Vietnam and of ending the war. The United States had not previously moved against the North Vietnamese forces and supplies in the Cambodian sanctuaries along the South

[1] "United States Foreign Policy for the 1970's," a report by President Richard Nixon to the Congress, February 18, 1970, p. 41.

Vietnamese border, he said, "because we did not wish to violate the territory of a neutral nation." But the Viet Cong and its allies from Hanoi had made a mockery of Cambodian neutrality. According to the President, they had used the 600 miles of frontier as "a vast enemy staging area and a spring-board for attacks on South Vietnam." [2] The purpose of the action taken, he said, was not to extend the war or to occupy Cambodian territory but to clean out the enemy's privileged bases. Once the North Vietnamese and Viet Cong could be driven out and their military supplies captured or destroyed, he promised, the American and South Vietnamese forces would be withdrawn.

Regardless of what the President might have said to explain the Cambodian venture, it would have brought down upon him an avalanche of criticism. But he exposed himself unnecessarily by seeming to take the offensive in a war that was supposed to be in the process of liquidation. Replying to critics who had suggested that his move against the sanctuaries would make him a one-term President, he declared: "Whether I may be a one-term President is insignificant compared to whether by our failure to act in this crisis the United States proved itself to be unworthy to lead the forces of freedom in this critical period in world history.

"I would rather be a one-term President and do what I believe was right than to be a two-term President at the cost of seeing America become a second-rate power and to see this nation accept the first defeat in its proud 190-year history." [3]

Here was a resurgence of manifest destiny along with an almost czarlike complex of acting for the free world. The President seemed to be saying that he alone, as Commander in Chief, carried the burden of wringing victory out of what

[2] Quoted in the *New York Times,* May 1, 1970, p. C2.
[3] Ibid.

was then widely acknowledged to be an ill-advised and unsuccessful presidential war. His new offensive, burgeoning suddenly out of retreat, alarmed his enemies and shocked many of his friends. Some of both concluded that the Nixon Doctrine had been exploded in a puff of rhetoric. By what he said, perhaps more than by what he did, the President enveloped the principal thesis of his foreign policy in a fog of confusion that is not likely to be lifted soon.

Actually there was a sound military reason for raiding the sanctuaries. For years the Communist foes of South Vietnam had been using this Cambodian territory to carry on the war. As the pressure on the Communist forces increased within South Vietnam, they made greater use of the sanctuaries just beyond the border. Until April 30 they were an island of immunity in a hotly contested war. Undoubtedly they did, as the President contended, add substantially to the American and South Vietnamese casualties and seriously complicate the problem of winding down the war. Only American restraint growing out of a desire not to widen the war had prevented earlier sweeps through the sanctuaries.

It is also true that the spring of 1970 presented a unique opportunity for the raids — an opportunity that had not existed before. In the previous years of the Vietnamese war Prince Norodom Sihanouk had held Cambodia in a precarious neutrality. American troops could not have cleaned out the sanctuaries without clashing openly with Sihanouk's forces, a move that would, of course, have driven him into the arms of Peking. But in March, 1970, Sihanouk had been deposed as head of state in a bloodless coup engineered by his premier and defense minister, Lieutenant General Lon Nol, and Prince Sisowath Sirik Matak, first deputy premier. Jean Lacouture suggests that the shift of power may have been a Machiavellian trick — that in order to avoid a direct confrontation with his Communist friends who were threatening his neutrality Sihanouk may have wanted to stand aside and let Lon Nol take on the chore of purging Cambodia of the Vietnamese presence, so that he could later come back to power with clean hands and a larger degree of freedom.[4] In any event, Sihanouk had entrusted Lon Nol with power three months before setting off on a long sojourn in France. Lon Nol had found the encroachments of the North Vietnamese upon Cambodia increasingly intolerable and had launched a campaign of resistance, with an appeal for help to the United States and various other countries.

In effect, therefore, the war had been widened before the President made his decision. All Indochina was involved. From the beginning of its invasion of South Vietnam, Hanoi had used Laotian as well as Cambodian territory to carry on its depredations. Indeed, the North Vietnamese Lao Dong, the Pathet Lao, and the South Vietnamese National Liberation Front had long been allied in a Communist conspiracy against the non-Communist elements in Indochina, and after the Cambodian coup their representatives welcomed Sihanouk's government-in-exile into the alliance at a meeting in South China. There is also evidence that previous plans had been laid for a war designed to bring about Communist control over Cambodia. Denis Warner reported details of the war plan from a notebook seized by the Cambodian authorities when they sacked the embassy of the Viet Cong in Phnom Penh on March 11. According to this source, Hanoi had decided before April, 1969, to expand its subversive activities in Cambodia and to send Communist armed forces into the countryside, but to work through Sihanouk if possible.[5] Apparently the ouster of Sihanouk brought the scheme into full operation. The question that President Nixon had to face was not whether the war would be widened, but what

---

[4] Lacouture's article in *Foreign Affairs Quarterly*, July, 1970, quoted in *Congressional Record*, August 31, 1970, p. S14708.
[5] Denis Warner in the *Washington Post*, July 13, 1970, p. A20.

the response of the United States would be to the widening that had already taken place.

In these circumstances, there was ample military reason for cleaning out the sanctuaries. Probably the raids into the Fishhook and Parrot's Beak areas yielded better results than any comparable use of the manpower involved could have done. As for the crossing of a neutral border, it is more realistic to view the event as a response to violations of international law than as a lawless act in and of itself. The North Vietnamese invasions of both Laos and Cambodia were flagrant violations of the 1962 Geneva Accords. The Americans went into Cambodia to right a wrong with at least the tacit approval of the government then in power at Phnom Penh — a government that had been appointed by Sihanouk and ratified by the Cambodian National Assembly. Premier Lon Nol later indicated that he would welcome the Americans back again if his own forces were unable to withstand the Communist assaults.

It is important to remember also that the Cambodian operation consisted of temporary raids; it was not an occupation. It lasted only two months. The penetration of American ground troops into Cambodia was restricted to a depth of twenty-one miles. As President Nixon noted in his report to the country after the last of the American troops had been withdrawn, "It was a limited operation for a limited period of time with limited objectives." [6] About 32,000 American troops and 48,000 South Vietnamese conducted search-and-destroy missions against a dozen of the most important North Vietnamese base areas in Cambodia. The bases proved to be sitting ducks. For the most part North Vietnamese and Viet Cong chose not to defend them; so it was a relatively simple matter to capture the supplies and ammunition and destroy the installations that were readily visible.

The President's report at the end of the operation es-

[6] Text in the *New York Times*, July 1, 1970, p. C16.

timated that 22,892 individual weapons and 2500 big crew-served weapons had been captured, along with more than 15 million rounds of ammunition, 14 million pounds of rice, 143,000 rockets, mortars, and recoilless rifle rounds designed for use against cities and bases, more than 199,552 anti-aircraft rounds, 5482 mines, 62,022 grenades, 83,000 pounds of explosives, and more than 435 vehicles. The President also claimed that more than 11,688 bunkers and other military structures were destroyed, that 11,439 men were killed and 2328 captured or detained.[7] While this appears to be a formidable toll exacted from the enemy, there is evidence that the statistics were carelessly gathered, with the object of making a good showing. Some observers in the area reported that the raiders found only 30 to 50 per cent of the military supplies that were actually stowed away in the sanctuaries. Other critics say that some American units crossed the border without knowing where they were going and with little understanding of what they should look for.

It is highly improbable, therefore, that any agreement will ever emerge as to the wisdom of ordering the raids. From the military point of view, the success of the operation appears to have been fairly well demonstrated. The enemy's capacity to launch an offensive was in some measure impaired. No doubt the capture of large stores of ammunition helped to bring about the subsequent reduction in American casualties. Perhaps it also justified the President's claim that Vietnamization was facilitated. But the great question to be resolved in Indochina was not a military one. The scales on which the Cambodian venture has to be weighed are, in the last analysis, more sensitive to political, diplomatic, psychological, and moral values.

It was apparent at the time that only wishful thinking underlay the President's assumption that the raids would "en-

[7] Ibid.

hance the prospects of a negotiated peace" and tend to shorten the war. There is no evidence in any part of our experience in Vietnam to suggest that the tough-minded rulers in Hanoi could be bludgeoned into negotiations. On the contrary, their obstinacy seemed to stiffen with adversity. In 1968 President Johnson finally gave up the bombing of North Vietnam because it had proved useless in softening the enemy for negotiations. In 1969 President Nixon began to liquidate the war, presumably on the same basis of reasoning. The objectives sought by the United States could not be won militarily, so American combat operations were subordinated to the training of South Vietnamese and the pursuit of an understanding that would allow complete evacuation of the U.S. forces from Vietnam. However it may be garbed in the rhetoric of peace, the excursion into Cambodia was a deviation from the course on which Washington had previously been set. The emphasis flipped back to military combat again. As previously noted, the President's explanation of the move assumed a win-the-war tone, and Washington appeared once again to be more concerned about a military coup than with the long-range aim of extricating the U.S.A. from a costly and seemingly futile land war on the continent of Asia.

One effect within the United States was to associate Mr. Nixon with the war more intimately than before. Until April 30, 1970, the tragedy in Vietnam had been Lyndon Johnson's war. But when Richard Nixon extended the fighting to Cambodia by resort to the same dubious executive authority that President Johnson had used in Vietnam and Laos, he seemed to inherit the whole shabby venture. The event brought mammoth protests and demonstrations in the United States. Many people felt that the President had arbitrarily compromised a withdrawal policy that had come to be accepted as a sort of general consensus. So the advantages that the President might have obtained from a resolute and determined policy of correcting his predecessor's mistakes in Vietnam were, in part at least, lost to him.

Congress was deeply troubled by the apparent widening of the war. In March, 1970, it had appeared that Congress and the Nixon administration might be approaching an understanding in regard to the Southeast Asian war in particular and as to use of the war power in general. Senator Charles McC. Mathias of Maryland was pushing a measure to repeal the Tonkin Gulf resolution and all the other acts which had seemed to welcome the President's use of our armed forces abroad at his own discretion. Majority Leader Mansfield and various others had joined in the movement, and the State Department had given its consent. A letter from Acting Assistant Secretary of State for Congressional Relations H. G. Torbert, Jr., to Chairman Fulbright of the Senate Foreign Relations Committee, written with the approval of Secretary Rogers, had indicated that the administration "is not depending on any of these resolutions as legal or constitutional authority for its present conduct of foreign relations, or its contingency plans." The department had then seemed to pledge that the executive branch would go to Congress for authority before launching any military venture in the future. The exact language of the document on this point was:

> Should a situation arise calling into play our treaty commitments or otherwise seriously and immediately affecting the vital United States interests in the areas affected by these Resolutions, we would wish to see Congress at that time fulfill its proper role under the Constitution in the decision-making process . . . Should circumstances warrant, and after consultation with appropriate committees and the congressional leadership, we might indeed seek further resolutions in fresh crises.[8]

[8] Copy of letter in Foreign Relations Committee files.

Senator Fulbright described the document as "the most enlightened and progressive and conciliatory and pleasant memorandum I've received in a long time." [9] On the surface at least the administration seemed willing to consult Congress in any future emergency calling for the use of armed forces and also to abide by the legislative judgment. But all this went out of the window when the President launched the Cambodian clean-out operation before mentioning it to Congress. The effect on Capitol Hill was to stiffen the determination to limit the war regardless of what the wishes of the White House might be.

Less than two weeks after the American troops crossed the Cambodian border, the Senate Foreign Relations Committee approved an amendment to a foreign military sales bill forbidding the expenditure of funds to keep U.S. military forces in Cambodia without congressional approval. The amendment was also designed to cut off funds for American forces training Cambodian soldiers or supporting Cambodian forces, to prohibit the payment of mercenaries for Cambodia, and to forbid American air support for Cambodian operations. After seven weeks of debate the Senate adopted the amendment a few hours after the last of the American troops came out of Cambodia. It was a belated gesture that was promptly voted down by the House, but it dramatically underlined the intensity of feeling in the Senate against the widened Indochinese war.

When the furor over the raids subsided, the Nixon administration reverted to its more conciliatory stance. On October 8 the President called for a "cease-fire in place" — an end to the shooting so that "we can set the stage for agreements on other matters." [10] It was significant that his proposal encompassed all of Indochina. "Conflicts in this region," he ex-

[9] *Washington Post* editorial, March 18, 1970.
[10] Text of the speech in the *New York Times*, October 8, 1970, p. L18.

plained, "are closely related." [11]   However vehement the previous disclaimers that the Cambodian raids had widened the war, the simple truth was that the war had been widened. So had American participation in it. The North Vietnamese were, of course, primarily responsible because they had used Cambodian territory for their arsenals. But the fact remained that, in the process of its attempted exit from Indochina, the United States had been sucked in a little deeper.

The raids also tended to link the United States to the fate of the Lon Nol regime in Phnom Penh. Without any previous collaboration, both were fighting the North Vietnamese in Cambodia. As the American forces were withdrawn, Washington faced a new problem of helping, or refusing to help, the new Cambodian regime maintain itself in power. If that shaky setup should topple, the Communists could make all Cambodia a sanctuary, thus complicating the problem of winding up the war in Vietnam. Of course the struggle for control of Cambodia would continue whether or not Washington lent a helping hand, and the United States had an obvious interest in the outcome. But if the United States should be lured into a new war for preservation of the independence of Cambodia, the whole Nixon policy of extricating our forces from the Vietnamese imbroglio would become a roaring farce.

In the face of this dilemma, Washington compromised. It initiated a policy of aiding the Lon Nol government by delivering 3000 captured Communist AK-47 rifles to Cambodian troops in an unmarked South Vietnamese military transport in May, 1970. By July a military assistance program for Cambodia was growing by "leaps and bounds." [12] Diplomat Robert Murphy, then chairman of the Foreign In-

[11] Ibid.
[12] Laurence Stern's dispatch from Phnom Penh in the *Washington Post*, July 6, 1970, p. A1.

telligence Advisory Board, and Gordon Gray, a member of the board, were dispatched to Phnom Penh along with a host of other officials and diplomats to assist in shaping an aid policy. The flow of supplies and weapons to Phnom Penh was at first financed by an earmarking of emergency funds for Cambodia. In August the State Department announced an additional program of military assistance amounting to $40 million, and in November the President asked that this figure be extended to $285 million. "It is essential," he told Congress in making the request, "that we supplement Cambodia's own efforts by providing resources which are critically needed to enable it to continue to defend itself." [13] Congress finally voted $230 million in economic and military aid to Cambodia while declaring that it could not be regarded as a commitment to the defense of that country.

The strings that Congress attached will be noted in more detail in Chapter 13. For the moment it is enough to observe that Congress was not satisfied by the President's assurance that Cambodia would not become another Vietnam. Gone was the assumption of 1964 that the President should have a free hand in dealing with such matters. Congress wrote into the law a prohibition against the use of American ground combat troops and advisers in Cambodia and more limited restrictions on the financing of third-party operations in that country. Although the Nixon administration accepted these restraints, they carried an implied rebuke to the President for having widened the war without the approval of Congress and a warning that he must not do it again.

In one area, however, the American entanglement with Cambodia remained untouched by these restrictions. U.S. air support for Cambodian forces went merrily on. When confronted by news dispatches from Phnom Penh, the Pentagon had acknowledged in June, 1970, that American pilots were

[13] *New York Times*, November 19, 1970, p. C11.

flying up to 100 miles inside Cambodia to attack Communist supply lines. Cambodian "air controllers" accompanied the American pilots to point out the enemy targets. Some of the planes refueled at Phnom Penh. Secretary of State Rogers explained this policy as a by-product of the American strategy in Vietnam. ". . . the main thrust of our policy," he said, "is to use our air force for the purpose of interdicting supply lines and communication lines to protect Americans in South Vietnam. That is our policy. Obviously, it may have a dual benefit — it may serve our purposes and at the same time serve the Cambodian government." [14] Rogers chose not to deny more candid reports from Phnom Penh that U.S. fighter-bombers were giving direct support to Cambodian ground forces. On July 5 Laurence Stern reported from Phnom Penh "massive American air operations directed from Saigon, which run the spectrum from B–52 strikes in Northeast Cambodia to photo-reconnaissance runs over Phnom Penh." [15] The overworked euphemism — "interdiction" — could not change the fact that the United States was participating in the Cambodian war, supplying the air power that was most vital to the Lon Nol forces. After his visit to Southeast Asia in January, 1971, Secretary of Defense Laird acknowledged that the United States was fighting a general air war in Cambodia.

Is this a true reflection of the Nixon Doctrine? That doctrine pledges the United States to stand by its treaty commitments, but we have no treaty commitment either to defend or to aid Cambodia. The Nixon Doctrine says that, in cases of nonnuclear aggression, "we shall furnish military and economic assistance when requested and as appropriate," but that "we shall look to the nation directly threatened to assume the primary responsibility of providing the manpower

[14] Murrey Marder in the *Washington Post,* June 26, 1970, p. 1.
[15] See Note 12.

for its defense." The Cambodian experience raises a grave question of whether the President was asserting a right to commit American air forces to combat operations whenever he thinks that a friendly government is in danger.

We cannot lose sight of the fact that the Cambodian operation is directly related to the war in Vietnam. Considering the nature of that struggle, it was probably impossible to prevent some kind of spillover in both Laos and Cambodia. This can be regarded as part of the price we must pay for having launched a presidential war on the continent of Asia to keep the two Vietnams apart. Once the United States was bogged down in this venture, with more than half a million men committed to the cause and no hope of a military victory, there could be no painless exit. The choice that President Nixon had to face, in the absence of any progress at the peace talks in Paris, was quiet withdrawal with the least possible friction or a stormy retreat, with occasional rearguard offensive operations, reprisals, and extension of the struggle into new areas. He cannot be judged as if he were writing on a clean slate.

Yet even while he was retreating from an overextended position the President seemed to cling adamantly to the role of self-appointed world policeman that had led his predecessor into that predicament. The result was to blur his intentions and confuse the doctrine he had enunciated as a general guide to his foreign policy. Despite his declaration that he did not wish to get drawn into a permanent defense of Cambodia, his actions created grave fears that he was traveling down that very road. Lyndon Johnson too had once been wary of a major military commitment on the continent of Asia. But military and economic aid granted to Vietnam had seemed to lead logically to the sending of advisers, to the large-scale training of the South Vietnamese troops, to the interdiction of supplies, to the mounting use of American ground troops, to the bombing of North Vietnam. In 1970 the American people were looking eagerly for reassurance that this evolution toward disaster would not be repeated, and they got an equivocal answer. While Congress put up a partial barrier against sliding into another war, it blandly ignored the air war that American pilots were carrying on in all of Indochina.

The result was a serious erosion of the Nixon Doctrine. The President seemed to slip back into the old pattern whenever it was convenient. A feeling of disillusionment spread at home and abroad. The Director of the United States Information Agency, Frank Shakespeare, acknowledged that the strike into Cambodia was a blow to American prestige in other countries. On the basis of an opinion poll that the USIA had commissioned, Mr. Shakespeare said: "There was a traumatic reaction in the world at large, particularly at the time it occurred." [16] The question of whether the setback in diplomatic circles and world opinion was offset by the military gains of the Cambodian operation may never be resolved. But it is clear that President Nixon's reversion to the big-stick role cost him dearly in terms of confidence and good will and befogged his image as a leader toward a new and more rational stance for the U.S.A.

[16] Terence Smith in the *New York Times*, December 21, 1970, p. C4.

VII

How to Irritate Friends
and Undermine Security

OUR CLOSEST FRIEND outside the NATO orbit and the Western Hemisphere is the Philippine Republic. As a former American colony, the Philippines have looked to Washington for help in many areas and for military protection. The United States has retained a sort of fatherly interest in the islands and their people. Here, if anywhere, it would seem, the role of protector-benefactor ought to bring satisfactory results. Yet the relations between the two countries have become troubled, as the frequent demonstrations in the vicinity of the United States Embassy in Manila attest.

Since Congress granted independence to the Philippines in 1946, the American intention of defending the islands in case of necessity has never been open to serious question. Such intent was implicit in the fact that the United States retained bases in the Philippines for "mutual protection." It was affirmed in the military bases agreement of 1947, the military assistance agreement of the same year, and the Mutual Defense Treaty of 1951. In the latter pact the two governments agreed that:

> Each party recognizes that an armed attack in the Pacific Area on either of the parties would be dangerous to its own

peace and safety and declares that it would act to meet the common dangers in accordance with its constitutional processes.[1]

This common defense policy in the Pacific was further tightened after the United States had established its bases in the Philippines. With American air and naval forces stationed in the islands, Secretary of State Dulles wrote the Philippine Foreign Secretary in 1954, "an armed attack on the Philippines could not but be also an attack upon the military forces of the United States. As between our nations, it is no legal fiction to say that an attack on one is an attack on both." [2] When President Eisenhower and President Garcia of the Philippines met in 1958 their communiqué added to the previous pledge the assurance that an attack upon the Philippines, while American forces were stationed there, would be "instantly repelled." President Johnson later renewed these pledges after state visits from President Macapagal and President Marcos.

Precisely what these commitments would mean in a crisis is still a mystery. Critics have read into them a determination on the part of the White House to take the decision out of the hands of Congress if military action for defense of the Philippines should seem necessary. Senator Fulbright complained that the presidential assurances tend "to negate altogether the whole concept of constitutional processes." [3] But James M. Wilson, Jr., Deputy Chief of Mission in Manila, repudiated that view when he appeared before the

[1] "United States Security Agreements and Commitments Abroad: The Republic of the Philippines," hearings before the Subcommittee on United States Security Agreements and Commitments Abroad of the Senate Committee on Foreign Relations, 91st Cong., 1st sess., part 1 (Washington: Government Printing Office, 1970), p. 6.
[2] Ibid.
[3] Ibid., p. 17.

Senate Subcommittee on United States Security Agreements and Commitments Abroad in 1969. His view was:

> We do not believe that the statements made by American Presidents and Secretaries of State in any way expand the treaty commitments. They simply recognize the fact that so long as U.S. forces are physically in the Philippines an attack on the Philippines would jeopardize their safety, and we would act to protect them. Our commitment to the security of the Philippines remains exactly as stated in the treaties themselves.[4]

The Filipinos, in their interpretations, tend to focus more on the fog in these agreements than on their reinforced implications. Officials in Manila have periodically sought changes in the treaty designed to make the promised American response more automatic in case of an attack. They would like to write into the United States–Philippines treaty the NATO language that very specifically pledges the participants to treat an attack upon one of them as an attack upon all. The United States has refused to go that far in the text of the treaty. But with officials in Washington repeatedly hinting that the presence of our troops in the Philippines has created a de facto watertight guarantee of security for the islands, the resulting confusion may someday prove extremely embarrassing.

The Philippine effort to secure a tighter United States guarantee seems strangely out of keeping with the simultaneous movement in Manila toward a more independent role in foreign policy. Secretary of Foreign Affairs Carlos P. Romulo is fond of talking about closer ties with the Philippines' Asian neighbors and less reliance upon the United States. He seems to be looking forward to a day when the Philippines will not need the shield now provided by the

[4] Ibid., p. 10.

American Navy and Air Force. In this he reflects the views of President Ferdinand E. Marcos. Having won reelection in November, 1969, through a campaign that promised tighter restriction of American military bases and investments in the Philippines, Marcos formally requested renegotiation of the bases agreement three days later. Disregarding the fact that one primary purpose of the bases is to protect the island republic, he has described them as an insult to the dignity of the Filipino people. Manila officials often appear to be more concerned about the bases as possible magnets for Chinese or Russian bombs than as defensive strongholds in case of war.

A serious question thus arises as to whether, even in the case of our good friend and protégé, the Philippines, we can maintain a satisfactory relationship while occupying immense bases in that country. The relationship has been enormously useful to both countries in terms of military policy. It has given the Philippine economy a substantial lift. Yet the bases remain a focal point of irritation, and there are many indications that opposition is more likely to increase than to diminish. Senate Majority Leader Mike Mansfield put the delicate issue in these words after a fact-finding trip to Asia:

> As nations whose futures are interwoven with the peace of the Pacific, the Philippines and the United States have a common interest in cooperating closely in the field of defense. In that sense, the U.S. bases in the Philippines are of great significance to both nations. In the end, however, the value of the bases is dependent not only on our willingness to support them, but also on Philippine acceptance of the arrangements which govern their usage . . .[5]

The United States' input into this arrangement has been rather staggering. Military and economic aid to the Philip-

[5] Quoted in Congressional Quarterly Fact Sheet, "Philippine Commitments," November 24, 1969, p. 4.

pines from 1946 to 1958 amounted to $2.023 billion. Although this includes large sums in the form of grants for the repair of war damage, it is indicative of an immense investment in joint defense. Military aid averaged $22.5 million annually from 1965 to 1969. In addition there are special types of aid and valuable tariff preferences.

As the new decade began about 51,000 Americans were in the Philippines, including 28,000 military personnel, 1400 civilians and 22,000 dependents. While the bases were operating in high gear because of the war in Vietnam they also employed about 50,000 Filipinos and generated an additional $150 million a year in foreign exchange. Operation of Clark Air Force Base alone was costing American taxpayers more than $270 million per year. It is the largest United States center for military aircraft in the Pacific, a so-called "heavy support" base. When Lieutenant General Francis C. Gideon, Commander of the 13th Air Force stationed at Clark, appeared before the Senate Foreign Relations Subcommittee on United States Security Agreements and Commitments Abroad in September, 1969, he noted that one of the major tasks of the base was the repair and maintenance of more than 800 aircraft of thirty-one types for service in Southeast Asia. The construction program carried out by the 13th Air Force in the Philippines, Thailand, and Taiwan from 1965 through 1969 cost $330 million. With some 17,000 airmen and officers and other personnel and dependents running to a total of about 65,000, Clark Air Base became the center of an immense military operation.

There are twenty American military stations in the Philippines. The principal ones, in addition to Clark Air Force Base, are: Subic Bay, which affords logistics support for the 7th Fleet, including complete ship-repair facilities, an air facility at Cubi Point, a hospital, magazine, naval magazine area, fuel depots, a transit area for cargo ships and tankers, and a fleet intelligence center; the United States Naval Communications Station in San Miguel; and Camp John Hay Air Force Base near Baguio, a communications center for airlift and air traffic control and a rest and recreation retreat. The Coast Guard also exercises administrative and operational control over five all-weather, long-range navigational systems known as LORAN (A) stations. Sangley Point, which had been used as a naval air station, was returned to the Philippines in 1970.

It is difficult for an ordinary legislator or citizen to judge how much of this enormous complex represents legitimate defense preparations and how much grandiose empire building. The story of the base at Mactan suggests, at the very least, a disturbing looseness about the operations. Mactan is 352 miles south of Clark. Originally the United States built it for the Philippines, retaining the right to use it in an emergency. When Clark Air Force Base became overloaded in 1965 because of the war in Vietnam, Washington asked and received permission to use Mactan. Part of the 463rd Tactical Airlift Wing was deployed there, and new facilities were constructed at a cost of $2.831 million. The facilities at Clark were also expanded, however, and the Mactan segments of the 463rd Airlift Wing were shifted there in 1968. Nevertheless, the Air Force continued to maintain 600 persons at Mactan at an operating cost of $4,385,000 for the fiscal year 1969.

In their investigation into security agreements and commitments abroad, Chairman Stuart Symington and his colleagues on the Senate subcommittee tried to find out why the base had not been closed. The following exchange is revealing of the mental processes which have kept many bases of dubious value in operation in different parts of the world:

MR. PAUL [*subcommittee counsel*]. In the light of this minimal function, could you tell us why Mactan, if I may ask a direct question, should continue to be operated as an American facility?

GENERAL GIDEON. Yes. We continue to evaluate these questions, and that one is being reevaluated at this time, as are all of the bases.

SENATOR SYMINGTON. With respect, General, I do not think that answer is quite responsive. Why do you keep the base open?

GENERAL GIDEON. Well, from my own point of view we keep it open because I am instructed to carry out the mission.

SENATOR SYMINGTON. Do you think it necessary to keep it open?

GENERAL GIDEON. Well, this would depend on the CINCPAC and Joint Chiefs of Staff's ultimate plans for this area. I really would not be competent to say long run whether they would require it or not . . .

SENATOR SYMINGTON. I do not mean to labor it, but let us get the facts. When did you start reevaluating it?

GENERAL GIDEON. Well, when I got there a year ago I looked and evaluated in a general sense the requirements of all our bases.

SENATOR SYMINGTON. Let me approach it in another way. Six flights a day. Do you think it worthwhile on the basis of six flights a day?

GENERAL GIDEON. My own personal opinion is that if this were the only reason for the retention of the base, no; that would not justify the retention of the base.

SENATOR SYMINGTON. Thank you, General. What could be the other reason or reasons?

GENERAL GIDEON. Well, if there were strategic requirements, if I may use that word.

SENATOR SYMINGTON. Escalation of the war, new fighting.

GENERAL GIDEON. Well, or general U.S. interest in this area.

SENATOR SYMINGTON. Thank you.

SENATOR FULBRIGHT. What do you mean by general U.S. interests? This could apply anywhere in the world.

GENERAL GIDEON. That is right, sir.

SENATOR SYMINGTON. Here is a base built for the Philippines.

We are paying for the base and pretend we need it because we have six flights a day of old planes like the C–124, and the pretty nearly as old C-133A's. If you put them into Clark you would save $5 million. We have a growing lot of troubles at home . . .

One can only wonder why you keep an expensive base, with hundreds of people, to handle six piston airplanes through it per day. It does not make much sense, especially as we are beginning to run out of money.[6]

The controversy over Mactan seemed to boil down to the fact that the Air Force was still spending lavishly on a useless base because of some vague feeling that sometime in the future it might conceivably be useful. In effect, the Air Force confessed its error of judgment by closing out its facilities at Mactan soon after the Senate hearing. But it was yielding to pressure in a specific case. Unfortunately, there is no evidence that the Pentagon has given up its general policy of empire building in distant lands.

The Symington subcommittee made very little progress in defining what our policy of maintaining bases in the Philippines ought to be. There was a good deal of talk at the hearings about the potential menace from Red China and the threat of a Communist uprising within the islands, but it was vague and unconvincing. Senator Symington pursued the subject with Rear Admiral Draper L. Kauffman, Commander in Chief, Pacific:

SENATOR SYMINGTON. What is the capacity from the military standpoint of the Red Chinese today in the Pacific to menace the Philippines . . .
ADMIRAL KAUFFMAN. I would say at the moment, sir, very small.
SENATOR SYMINGTON. General, what would you say?

[6] "United States Security Agreements and Commitments Abroad: The Philippines," pp. 121–122.

GENERAL GIDEON. Very small, very small.

SENATOR SYMINGTON. But you say it is the principal threat.

ADMIRAL KAUFFMAN. Of the threats that exist, I would say it is the principal threat; yes, sir.

SENATOR SYMINGTON. What you are really saying, militarily speaking, is there is no threat to the Philippines, are you not?

ADMIRAL KAUFFMAN. If by the word "threat" —

SENATOR SYMINGTON. I am only using your word, not my word.

ADMIRAL KAUFFMAN. I think I was using it as a longer term implication perhaps, sir, than perhaps just right now.

SENATOR SYMINGTON. What do you mean exactly?

ADMIRAL KAUFFMAN. Well, I would say when the Chinese Communists have perfected the use of a nuclear weapon that threat would increase.

SENATOR SYMINGTON. I do not want to labor it, but you have a fine air force in Formosa which the American taxpayer helped pay for. You have the U.S. Air Force in Okinawa. You have our air force in the Philippines, and you also have the 7th Fleet. So when you say that the principal threat to the Philippines is Communist China, without getting too syllogistic about it, what you are actually saying is that today there is no threat to the Philippines except an internal threat. Is that not a fair extrapolation?

ADMIRAL KAUFFMAN. Yes, sir, using the word "today." [7]

Since the Communist insurgents in the Philippines known as Huks number only about 400, with a few thousand others classified as supporters and sympathizers, out of a population of 37 million, the internal menace does not appear to be especially serious. It would not, of course, justify the United States in maintaining its formidable military presence in the Philippines. In the absence of any comprehensive military explanation of the Philippine bases at the Symington subcommittee hearings, Senator Fulbright advanced the argument that their only purpose was to guarantee that the

[7] Ibid., pp. 60–61.

United States would be involved in any trouble that might develop between China and the Philippines. But this was doubtless intended as a baiting observation. James W. Wilson, Jr., noted that "having those bases there is a means of making it possible for the United States to operate in that part of the world and this is also in the Philippines' interest." The major questions are whether this country is paying too high a price "to operate in that part of the world" and whether the net effect of such operations is a contribution to peace or to the exacerbation of military rivalries which seem to keep the world teetering on the edge of war.

One part of the cost which cannot be readily dismissed is the persistent, large-scale crime directed at the American military. Colonel Ernest W. Pate, Commander of the 6th Air Division at Clark Air Force Base, told the Symington subcommittee that losses at Clark from crime and corruption, involving Americans as well as Filipinos, amounted to $255,-336.85 in 1968. Thefts and unexplained losses of property became so widespread that officials at the base found it necessary to create a Philippine constabulary to aid the regular security police in patrolling the base perimeter, providing armed escort for high-value cargoes, and controlling irate Filipino demonstrators. During the first eight months of 1968, seventy-one Americans required emergency medical treatment as a result of assaults and armed robberies in Angeles City, which has been described as a "rathole honkytonk of vice adjoining the Clark gate." [8] One of the victims was beaten to death with a gear-shift lever. The following details from Colonel Pate's report constitute a rather grim backdrop to the base problem in the Philippines:

In August [1968], assaults increased over the preceding month by 20%; armed robberies increased 25%; and the num-

[8] Ibid., p. 207. The quote is from *Fortune* magazine.

ber of robberies involving injuries increased 33%. In the first week of September, attacks on Americans escalated sharply in Angeles City. Six victims of unprovoked and random rock throwing attacks required medical care. On 1 September, USAF security police broke up a fight between two U.S. Servicemen and took them into custody. City policemen took one of the men from our patrol at gunpoint. He was threatened with a cocked weapon and suffered injuries to the head and chest from blows with a rifle butt. On 5 September, an airman was arrested for a minor traffic violation and the city policeman removed him from his car and marched him to police headquarters with a cocked pistol at his head. The airman was held for about four hours and forced at gunpoint to sign an incriminating statement before he was released on 7 September. Two Americans disputed an overcharge for a jeepney ride and they were threatened with an ice pick by the driver who was joined by other Filipinos brandishing carbines. When they fled a shot was fired and one American sought protection from a housing subdivision security guard whom he mistook for a city policeman. Instead, he was twice beaten unconscious with a rifle butt and required emergency treatment for severe scalp wounds.[9]

The mounting assaults and the failure of Angeles City authorities to offer any better protection led officials at the base to impose a curfew on American personnel in the city. An economic blight thus fell on the city's night life, producing a new type of smoldering resentment. Conditions grew worse. A city policeman provoked an argument with a Filipino driver of an American school bus; some of the youngsters intervened and two of them were assaulted; all six were hustled off to the city jail where they were held for three and a half hours. City officials issued permits for demonstrations against the base and on two occasions thousands of hostile

[9] Ibid., p. 148.

students and others blocked the entrance to Clark, delivered anti-American speeches, and hanged various American officials in effigy. The Philippine constabulary intervened to keep the events from degenerating into violence and complete chaos.

A few weeks later the Angeles City Council declared certain Clark officials persona non grata to Angeles City, abolished the base-community council, which had been trying to restore order, and declared the city off limits to all American nationals at Clark. Checkpoints were established for all vehicles entering or leaving the base as if it were hostile territory in time of emergency. Another demand of the city council was for reexamination and revision of all United States–Philippines treaties and agreements pertaining to bases and mutual security "so as to assert her [the Philippines'] sovereignty and to eliminate all vestiges of colonialism." The city fathers also called for replacement of all American base commanders by Filipinos and the relinquishment of law and order to Filipino security forces.

Crime at some of the other bases in the Philippines was less flagrant than at Clark but not exactly minimal. Admiral Kauffman testified before the Symington subcommittee that Subic Bay had seventy-three "major incidents" in the year ending August 1, 1969 — which breaks down into forty-nine robberies and twenty-four acts of violence, counting only the crimes of Filipinos against Americans. Some officials believe that the especially dismal record at Clark Air Force Base is due, at least in part, to the fact that it is in Huk territory, but this scarcely minimizes the problem. The bases are supposed to add to the security of American interests in the Far East, but they themselves are a source of insecurity in the areas where they are located. Lieutenant General Robert H. Warren, the Deputy Assistant Secretary of Defense for Military Assistance and Sales, noted that military assistance to the Philippines has averaged $22.5 million annually in recent years and expressed the belief that it is paid in part to protect the U.S. forces in the islands. "From whom?" Senator Symington asked. The general replied: "Internally, sir; to maintain internal security and stability and, thereby, make our activities over there more secure."

"In other words," Symington suggested, "we are paying the Philippine Government to protect us from the Philippine people who do not agree with the policies of the Government or do not like Americans."

"To a degree, yes, sir," [10] General Warren acknowledged.

Further illumination on how the overextension of our military presence in a friendly land has produced negative dividends is evident in the story of PHILCAG. The Philippine Civic Action Group consisted of an engineer construction battalion and medical and civic action teams, about 2200 men including a small security force, sent to Vietnam in 1966. Ostensibly it was the Filipinos' contribution to the war and was widely applauded in Washington as an example of "free Asian" support for the United States' efforts in Vietnam. President Johnson expressed his "deep satisfaction" and the thanks of the American people. President Marcos of the Philippines, addressing a joint session of Congress in Washington, declared: "Our object must be to hold the line in Vietnam and at least roll back Communist power behind the 17th parallel." [11] But they didn't tell us at the time that the United States was paying in part for Manila's timid gesture.

Like so many other cracks in the cement of American-Filipino friendship, the subsidies connected with PHILCAG came to light in the Symington subcommittee's investigation of American commitments abroad. Majority Leader Mans-

[10] Ibid., p. 245.
[11] Ward Just in the *Washington Post*, November 30, 1969, p. B6.

field was concerned about the origin of the engineer battalion:

> SENATOR MANSFIELD. May I ask a question and interpolate there?
>
> Mr. Minister, did the Filipinos dispatch this battalion of theirs, these engineer troops, to Vietnam on the basis of their own initiative or on the basis of a request and pressure from the U.S. Government?
>
> MR. WILSON. I must rely on this, Senator Mansfield, on my recollection of the records since I was not there personally at the time.
>
> To the best of my knowledge it was a combination of three things: There was an active interest on the part of the U.S. Government in bringing forces from other nations into the conflict in Vietnam. As part of this program, discussions were held with the Government of the Philippines just as they were with the Government of Thailand and the Government of Korea, and the Government of Australia, and the Government of New Zealand.
>
> In addition, the Government of South Vietnam approached the Government of the Philippines directly and asked if they would make a contribution.
>
> Finally, there was a considerable body of opinion in the Philippines itself which felt that a contribution should be made . . .
>
> As you perhaps recall, Senator, President Macapagal originally was talking of sending a combat-type force. President Marcos, when he was then leader of the Liberal Party, had gone strongly on record as opposing sending any force at all. It was only after he became President and had studied the situation further that he modified his position to the extent of saying "No, I will not send, I will not permit the sending of, any combat forces. But I will get behind the idea of sending a civic action force." This would be doctors, nurses, civic action teams, construction engineers, and also its own indigenous security force.

The cost to American taxpayers of this dubious showing of the Philippine flag in Vietnam came high. According to information supplied by the Defense Department, bonuses paid to members of PHILCAG out of American funds ranged from ten cents a day for privates to six dollars a day for a brigadier general plus overseas allowances. The United States also provided equipment, general supplies, gasoline and oil, maintenance, transportation, and so forth. The total outlay of American tax funds for PHILCAG has been officially estimated at $36 million. Senator Fulbright concluded from the information supplied by State and Defense Department witnesses that "all we did was go over and hire their soldiers in order to support our then administration's view that so many people were in sympathy with our war in Vietnam. And we paid a very high price for it." [12]

When the details of the PHILCAG arrangement were disclosed by the Symington subcommittee, President Marcos' office issued a statement saying that "it would be erroneous to describe the United States' contribution as a subsidy in any form or as a fee in return for the sending of the Philippine contingent." Official Washington was well aware of official Manila's reluctance to acknowledge the connection between the payments made and the dispatch of the troops. But the facts would not evaporate. Comptroller General Elmer B. Staats later substantiated the information released by the investigating senators, although investigators for the Philippine Senate insisted that there was no connection between PHILCAG and the American subsidies. So the net effect of the PHILCAG operation was to embarrass both governments and further to discourage hope of genuine American-Philippine cooperation in promoting mutual security.

[12] "United States Security Agreements and Commitments Abroad: The Philippines," p. 261.

Incidentally, the Philippines had a combat battalion that had been especially equipped and prepared for service, if necessary, under the Southeast Asia Treaty Organization. The United States supported this unit under its military assistance program with the object of helping to prepare SEATO for any emergency that might arise. When the show-down came, however, President Marcos refused to let these or any other combat troops be used. SEATO proved to be an illusory sort of commitment so far as Manila was concerned, but of course the United States itself had not called a SEATO conference for determination of the policy to be followed in Southeast Asia. Having entered Vietnam on a go-it-alone basis and having antagonized the Philippines by excessive military presumptions, the Johnson administration was reduced to begging for the pretense of cooperation for which it offered handsome rewards. A strange sort of security partnership indeed!

The alliance between the United States and the Philippines is a natural product of history, common interests, and long-standing friendly ties. It is a relationship that ought to be perpetuated in the interests of both countries. The Philippines needs American protection, financial aid, economic support, and encouragement in the development of a viable democratic society. The United States needs both naval and air bases in the Philippines for support of its Pacific policies. If there is to be a general or partial liquidation of U.S. bases in the Far East, those in the Philippines probably ought to be the last to go. Despite this very natural and legitimate partnership, however, the relations have been strained by excessive military proliferation and the type of arrogance that only the uniformed services in a foreign land seem capable of.

Close observers of the Philippine scene say that even the number of Americans in uniform in the islands is less troublesome than the tendency of some to throw their weight around. Attention in the U.S.A. tends to be focused on the crimes against our servicemen, but the Filipinos are more impressed by the cases in which soldiers abuse civilians. When a reckless GI shoots a civilian or a general's wife kills a pedestrian and speeds into an American base in order to claim immunity to trial in a Philippine court, a wave of resentment flows out through the community. In some minor cases the local anger seems out of proportion to the seriousness of the offense. Another source of friction is the constant flaunting of American affluence in the face of the relative poverty of the islands. American servicemen have gone to the Philippines expecting to be welcomed as friends and protectors and discovered that, to the average Filipino, they are a pain in the neck. Basic friendliness for America and what it stands for is still strong in the Philippines, but the insensitivity of a nuclear-armed Gulliver in the land of the Lilliputians, militarily speaking, has raised some grave questions about future relationships.

Even under the most favorable circumstances our overly inflated policy of building and maintaining military bases abroad has produced risks that, in the end, may overbalance the supposed short-run advantages. There is more than a little truth in the belief that the country that seeks its security with cavalier unconcern about the security of others is in danger of losing it.

VIII

Our Military Liaison with Spain

THE PRACTICE OF BUILDING American military bases at strategic points all over the globe, with little regard for the consequences, reached its culmination in Spain. From the beginning the tie between the two countries has been one of strained convenience. Generalissimo Franco's regime in Madrid was eager to obtain military supplies and the prestige that would flow from an alliance of any kind with the United States. The White House was willing to brush aside the widespread distrust of Franco in this country and Europe in order to round out its chain of bases deemed essential by the military to its world policing role.

The first agreement was signed in 1953, one of the most frigid years of the cold war. Secretary Dulles and the Pentagon were especially eager to establish Strategic Air Command bases in Spain as a means of buttressing the defenses of Western Europe in the period of transition from bombers to missiles armed with nuclear warheads. They obtained for the United States the right "to develop, maintain and utilize for military purposes, jointly with the government of Spain, such areas and facilities in territory under Spanish jurisdiction as may be agreed upon." In return the United States assumed an obligation to provide Spain with at least "the minimum requirements for equipment necessary to the defense of Spanish territory."

The era of senatorial abdication was still in full flower. Secretary of State Dulles had met with congressional leaders to discuss the most suitable way of handling international agreements, with specific reference to the prospective deal for Spanish bases. Dulles later informed President Eisenhower that "some of the Senators expressed the view that such agreements may be concluded by the President without further authority, particularly as future commitments for funds are subject to Congressional appropriation. No one dissented from that view." [1] With such lack of concern on Capitol Hill, the Eisenhower administration did not ask for the advice or consent of the Senate. Under the executive agreement thus concluded the United States spent, during the next fifteen years, $395.6 million for the construction of military bases in Spain and $793 million in connection with their operation. In addition the United States gave Spain economic aid amounting to $1.333 billion and military aid totaling $619.7 million.

Torrejon Air Base near Madrid became headquarters for the 16th Air Force, the 401st Tactical Fighter Wing, a Military Airlift Command unit, a Strategic Air Command support group, and numerous communications and support units. Moron Air Base near Seville has been used chiefly by an air-sea rescue squadron. Zaragoza Air Base in northeastern Spain was put in caretaker status in 1969. All three of the air bases are deemed useful for the augmentation of U.S. forces in case of a general war. Rota Naval Base near Cadiz has served primarily as a home port for the tender that serv-

[1] "United States Security Agreements and Commitments Abroad: Spain and Portugal," hearings before the Subcommittee on United States Security Agreements and Commitments Abroad of the Senate Committee on Foreign Relations, 91st Cong., 2nd sess., Part 11 (Washington: Government Printing Office, 1970), p. 2344.

ices Polaris-equipped nuclear submarines. In addition to these major bases, the United States built a petroleum, oil, and lubricant pipeline that connects all four of the bases, along with oil storage tanks, an ammunition storage depot, and various communications facilities.

Some of the facilities in Spain were originally designed to take the place of those in Morocco. The United States had acquired three SAC bases in Morocco in 1950 when that country was still a French protectorate. After Morocco became independent, President Eisenhower agreed to withdraw the American military forces by 1963 when the B–47 bomber was to be phased out. That seemed to be a good argument for more facilities in Spain. At Rota the military installed sensitive equipment for communicating between Washington and its Polaris submarines patrolling in the Mediterranean area. Actually, however, the Americans did not give up their similar facilities in Morocco. The bases were turned over to Morocco, but 1700 Americans were allowed to remain at the huge Kenitra base complex and to use its communications equipment under the pretense that they were training Moroccans.

When this story was brought to light by the Symington subcommittee, it produced some indignant outbursts. Senator Fulbright referred to it as "a classic case of proliferation. If we keep this up," he added, "we will be in every country in the world. We are in nearly every country now, and how do we stop it, especially when you want it all kept classified and thus we can't talk about it on the Senate floor? How in the world do you ever bring this kind of proliferation to an end?" [2]

The Symington subcommittee drew this conclusion:

[2] "United States Security Agreements and Commitments Abroad: Morocco and Libya," hearings before the Subcommittee on United States Security Agreements and Commitments Abroad of the Senate Committee on Foreign Relations, 91st Cong., 2nd sess., Part 9 (Washington: Government Printing Office, 1970), p. 1975.

The Naval Base at Rota was a marginal facility when it was built in the 1950's. In the 1960's, it was given the mission of replacing the communications facilities which were presumably being phased out of bases in Morocco. This mission of Rota became redundant when the communications facilities continued in Morocco. At the same time, a Polaris tender was anchored in Rota's harbor, and the support of Polaris submarines thereupon became the major justification for extending the Spanish base agreement.[3]

The pact with Franco underwent a significant upgrading when it was renewed for five years in 1963. In return for continued use of the bases the United States supplied an additional $100 million in military aid for Spain and tightened up the mutual defense arrangement. Franco had sought a security guarantee similar to that in the NATO alliance. The U.S. negotiators were not willing to go that far, but they compromised with a strong hint that the United States would go to the defense of Spain if that country should be attacked. The first version of the agreement had been nebulous on this point. To clarify the second version, Secretary of State Rusk and the Spanish Foreign Minister, Fernando Maria Castiella, signed a joint declaration in which the two governments "reaffirmed their recognition of the common dangers, and their determination to maintain a close working relationship on all matters affecting their common interests and security." The statement went a long way toward marrying the American and Spanish defense systems. Its most significant paragraph reads as follows:

The United States Government reaffirms its recognition of the importance of Spain to the security, well-being and de-

[3] "Security Agreements and Commitments Abroad," report of the Senate Subcommittee on Security Agreements and Commitments Abroad, December 21, 1970, 91st Cong., 2d sess. (Washington: Government Printing Office), p. 11.

velopment of the Atlantic and Mediterranean areas. The two governments recognize that the security and integrity of both Spain and the United States are necessary for the common security. A threat to either country, and to the joint facilities that each provides for the common defense, would be a matter of common concern to both countries, and each country would take such action as it may consider appropriate within the framework of its constitutional processes.[4]

Though vague and open to varying interpretations, this language is similar to the wording of the Southeast Asia defense treaty (SEATO) used by President Johnson as the source of his authority for the war in Vietnam. In both cases there is an implied promise to meet any common danger in accord with constitutional processes. In the case of the pledge to Spain, however, the agreement was never submitted to the Senate for its advice and consent to ratification. The Kennedy administration took upon itself the responsibility of establishing a "common security" policy with Spain without giving the Senate an opportunity to weigh the dangers involved, and the Senate again failed to assert its prerogative.

There is no way of knowing how this pledge might have been interpreted if Spain had been attacked, but the potential is alarming. One has to remember that the bases in question do not belong to the United States. Despite the enormous sums poured into their development by the U.S., they are Spanish property and this country has only the right to use them temporarily — presumably so long as Spain does not claim them for her own use. What would have happened if the chronic friction between Spain and Britain over Gibraltar had flared into hostilities? It seems inconceivable that the United States would have joined Spain in a war against the British, but Spain would presumably have claimed the joint

[4] *United States Treaties and Other International Agreements*, Vol. 14 (Washington: Government Printing Office, 1964), p. 1406.

bases for her own use. The Americans would have had to evacuate the bases or to remain under extremely precarious and embarrassing conditions. It must be assumed also that Spain would use the equipment she has obtained from the U.S. in any such war. Washington would thus be in the position of having contributed mightily to the cause of a dictatorial government — a cause that, in this instance, would run counter to our own basic interests.

Suppose, on the other hand, that the United States should become involved in hostilities in Europe or the Mediterranean area! Would the Spanish bases be available to us in such circumstances? During the Arab-Israeli war in 1967 Spanish officials are reported to have asked the U.S. not to use the bases, except for flights to evacuate people who might be in danger.[5] Obviously Spain, fearing that the U.S. might be drawn into a Middle East war, wanted to remain aloof from it. This is wholly understandable, but it suggests that in any future emergency Spain would dictate whether the bases were to be used and, if so, how. The current version of the agreement calls for consultation between the two governments on use of the bases if war should break out. Clearly the Franco regime has a veto on their use during any emergency. The U.S. could scarcely ignore any restrictions that Spain might lay upon the use of "joint" bases on Spanish soil, and if it should the result might be war in Spain itself.

When the 1963 version of the agreement came up for renewal in 1968, it ran into heavy weather on both sides of the Atlantic. In Spain there was resentment because of a belief that the Americans were using bases on Spanish soil solely for their own purposes and a feeling that Spain was not being treated as an equal. Friction between American personnel on the bases and the adjacent communities added to the background of resentment. At Rota a speeding sailor had

[5] Neil Sheehan in the *New York Times*, August 14, 1970.

run over and killed four members of a family walking on a roadside, and more than a dozen other fatal traffic accidents involving Spaniards were reported. Some Rotanos feared that nuclear missiles at the base would explode or leak radioactivity.[6] Many Americans living in Spain were also conscious of deep hostility toward the pact among the people because of their belief that it served to prop up the Franco regime and thus perpetuate its power.

In the United States there was also much concern over the prestige and military strength that Franco derived from the agreement. Citizens were especially puzzled by the participation of American troops in joint maneuvers aimed at theoretical rebellion in Spain. On several occasions American troops in Germany were flown to Spain for these practice operations. On at least one occasion Americans in uniform were reported to have parachuted into northern Spain to "round up and destroy guerrillas." The hostile forces against which these practice maneuvers were supposed to be aimed were not deemed to be foreign invaders but anti-Franco Spaniards.[7] The use of Americans in this kind of war game was stopped when its political implications were brought into focus, but it illustrates the extremes to which the military will push its policing operations.

Critics in the United States were especially fearful that the Nixon administration might extend the American "commitment." Madrid complained that the mutual defense arrangement was altogether too flabby and uncertain, but the risk it involved often seemed frightening on this side of the water. "Some foreign engagements, such as our bases agreement with Spain," said a report of the Senate Foreign Relations Committee, "form a kind of quasi-commitment, unspecified as to their exact import but, like buds in springtime, ready, under

[6] Richard Eder's report from Rota, *New York Times*, June 27, 1969, p. C2.
[7] Flora Lewis in the *Washington Post*, June 14, 1969, p. A25.

the right climatic conditions, to burst into full bloom." [8]

For domestic consumption, the State Department insisted that the Rusk-Castiella declaration did not involve a commitment of the United States to the defense of Spain. But the language had been suggested by the then Spanish ambassador who took its substance from the defense treaties between the United States and its allies. Since the United States had accepted this skillful synthesis of its defense treaties, Spain had a right to assume that an alliance for mutual defense was intended. It is also interesting to note that when the American negotiator discussed this declaration with the Spanish delegates in 1970 he too acknowledged that it constituted a defense commitment, in sharp conflict with what the State Department was saying to the American public. In a closed session of the Senate Foreign Relations Committee, Under Secretary of State Johnson was asked why the 1963 language was dropped if, as he had contended, it involved no commitment. He replied:

> . . . let me say during our discussions with the Spanish in their efforts to get language which I would interpret as a commitment they pushed very, very strongly for getting this language that was in the Joint Declaration of 1963. I have said that we could not do that without entering into a mutual defense treaty, and this was a road that we did not want to go." [9]

The 1963 declaration was not a commitment when the old agreement was being defended before the American people, but it was a commitment when the negotiators were trying to avoid its renewal. Johnson attempted to explain this inconsistency by saying that the State Department wished to eliminate the declaration in deference to the Foreign Relations

[8] *New York Times,* April 18, 1969, p. 1.
[9] "Spanish Base Agreement," hearing before the Senate Foreign Relations Committee, 91st Cong., 2nd sess., August 26, 1970, p. 56.

Committee. The committee was indeed hostile toward the declaration, but it was not conjuring up a bugaboo without substance. Its distrust rested on substantial evidence that the Executive Branch had created an alliance of sorts without the advice and consent of the Senate. In these circumstances the State Department's adamant denials that any commitment was involved had the ring of an excuse for not sending the new pact to the Senate. The executive branch submits to the Senate treaties on many relatively trivial matters from taxation to extradition, but in this delicate sphere of national security it insisted on acting without resort to the senatorial safety valve.

While negotiations for renewal of the agreement were still going on in 1968, they were further complicated by a furor over a sort of back-door "commitment" given to the Spanish negotiators by the Pentagon. Madrid had presented outrageous demands, allegedly asking $1.2 billion in aid over five years and a tighter pledge that the United States would defend Spain in case of attack. No ground for a compromise was in sight. In an effort to get the negotiations off dead center, Secretary Rusk suggested to Foreign Minister Castiella, when they met on October 17, 1968, in a farewell call by the latter, that military leaders of the two countries attempt to work out common strategic concepts. This was acceptable to Castiella, and the two officials also agreed in principle that they wished to renew the bases agreement and that after the military chiefs had completed their discussions diplomats on the two sides would undertake to clear up any remaining problems.

General Earle G. Wheeler, Chairman of the Joint Chiefs of Staff, was sent to Madrid to initiate these military discussions on the basis of a letter of instructions from Secretary Rusk. There he met with General Diez-Alegria and agreed to divide the military talks into three phases: First, they would try to identify military threats within a zone of common strategy that could affect the two countries either jointly or singly; second, they would study tasks and missions each country should undertake to counteract threats affecting both; third, they would study planning, basing, training, and equipment needed for those missions. As a result of these meetings, Wheeler prepared a truly remarkable document that he presented to General Diez-Alegria as well as to the Pentagon and the State Department. His conclusions, as later disclosed by the Symington subcommittee, were:

> . . . I believe it desirable that military representatives of our two countries explore the military measures which should be taken by our respective countries acting in concert to enhance the military capabilities of our Armed Forces to deter or defeat threats to our security. Our forthcoming military discussions on our respective contributions to mutual security should carefully examine in detail those elements which will enhance our military posture.
>
> . . . we should agree to joint military planning arrangements between our staffs and subordinate military commanders which will enable us to share defense missions and tasks in the most effective manner in meeting the mutual threat . . .
>
> The presence of the Russian fleet in the Mediterranean [deleted] only serves to emphasize the desirability for Spain and the United States to continue our mutual defense relationship. Together we can provide powerful maritime and air forces capable of countering such potential aggression. [Deleted] serve to increase the possibility of aggression below the nuclear level and provide the USSR with a means of gaining a foothold in Western Europe through limited aggression. Together we can frustrate such efforts in Iberia . . .
>
> In light of [deleted] the U.S. agrees that Spain is now more vulnerable to limited aggression due to the evolution of [deleted] strategy and equipment. An isolated Spain will mark Spain as a special target of this strategy. It is in the interests of

both our nations to insure that this is not permitted to happen.

By the presence of U.S. forces in Spain, the U.S. gives Spain a far more visible and credible security guarantee than any written document.[10]

At first this amazing document appears to have been reviewed by the State Department without any sense of alarm. General Wheeler thought he had acted within the guidance Secretary Rusk had given him, and no one challenged him on any vital point for several weeks. Then the Deputy Secretary of Defense, Paul H. Nitze, told Wheeler that he had inaccurately assumed that the military was to wrap up a complete package in regard to the bases for presentation to the two governments. He had grandly talked about political as well as military relations between the two countries as if a security alliance had been taken for granted.

Wheeler had turned over the detailed military negotiations to General David Burchinal, Deputy U.S. Commander in Chief, Europe, and passed along to him the instructions from Secretary Rusk as well as Wheeler's own memorandum. At the behest of Nitze, Wheeler modified his instructions to Burchinal in a cable on December 3. When the first memorandum of Burchinal's discussion with General Diez-Alegria reached Washington, the outlines of what the military was prepared to do to aid Spain in the case of peripheral threats was somewhat more clearly defined. John Leddy, the Assistant Secretary of State for European Affairs, sounded the alarm in the State Department, and the military was asked to modify an embarrassing overstatement.

It is not easy, however, to undo what has once been done in diplomatic negotiations. Any request for a change in the language that Burchinal had approved would involve a loss of face on his part in further negotiations with the Spanish

[10] "Security Agreements and Commitments" (Note 1), pp. 2363, 2356.

generals. Burchinal was summoned back to Washington and worked with representatives of the State and Defense Departments to refute or neutralize the unfortunate concession without changing the original language. The outcome was the attachment of a preamble to the second Burchinal memorandum that said:

> The present document on tasks and missions, as well as the previous discussions at the military level, are not necessarily the views of the Governments of Spain and the United States nor do they imply intergovernmental understandings or commitments between the two countries.[11]

Work on this second memorandum had begun early in January, 1969, but it was not signed until February 27. Two days earlier Flora Lewis had broken the story of the generals' tentative hidden commitment, with widespread repercussions. Later the Symington subcommittee examined the entire incident in rather extensive detail. With Secretary Rusk no longer in charge (he had been replaced by William P. Rogers when the Nixon administration came in) the State Department seemed chiefly concerned about the generals' encroachment upon the diplomatic function and their willingness to look upon a challenge to Spain from Algeria or her own African colonies as involving the security of the United States. On Capitol Hill, however, the sense of alarm that grew out of the incident was related almost entirely to the military acknowledgment that 25,000 Americans in Spain (military personnel and their dependents) were a better security guarantee than a treaty could be.

Senator Fulbright asked Wheeler if he had intended to say that the presence of American troops in Spain was "more credible than if we had a formal treaty." His question led to this exchange:

[11] Ibid., p. 2317.

GENERAL WHEELER. What I was driving at there, Mr. Chairman, and the point which I stressed when I talked to the Spaniards [was] that the presence of our forces and our people there, I thought, acted as a deterrent to aggression against them, that lacking the presence of our people, this is the same in Germany, that a piece of paper is just a piece of paper.

SENATOR FULBRIGHT. General, I am inclined to agree with you, . . . and I think going on with this [the base agreement with Spain] is the equivalent of an extension of NATO if not more so, because of the undertakings that we make.

Is alignment with Spain in U.S. interest? . . . Here is one of the oldest and most entrenched military dictatorships in the world today. Maybe that is all right. But it appears to me that this is such an important obligation that it ought to be submitted in the regular course under our Constitution as a treaty and let the United States decide if it wishes to obligate itself, to undertake the defense of Spain, under any and all circumstances, which I think you do by your language here. I think it ought to be a decision of the whole country and not a decision of the Secretary of State and the Joint Chiefs and a few people like this . . .

GENERAL WHEELER. Mr. Chairman, I am not competent to respond to your comment. This is a matter, it seems to me, that should be addressed at the highest levels of the executive department and of the Congress.[12]

But the general had felt competent to assure the Spanish that they would have an American guarantee of security regardless of what the agreement on bases might say. The military had taken advantage of the long leash given it by Secretary Rusk to offer a secret understanding, which, if it had been allowed to stand, seemed to pledge the good faith of the United States to the defense of Spain as long as American troops might remain in that country. And, viewed in the light of the joint military exercises authorized by the Pen-

[12] Ibid., pp. 2360–2361.

tagon, this could readily be extended to defense of the Franco regime. The incident stands as a classical example of the dangers of entrusting delicate negotiations involving the national security to the military, even on an "ad referendum" basis, as the diplomats say.

After the Nixon administration took over the negotiations, Secretary Rogers indicated that under no circumstances would he agree to any additional security commitment to Spain. Numerous differences remained, but in June, 1969, the bases agreement was extended for fifteen months so as to allow ample time for the negotiation of a longer-range pact. Foreign Minister Castiella took advantage of the occasion to declare that "the era of foreign military bases has ended" and that any new agreement must cover "economic, scientific, technical and cultural aspects" and recognize Spain as "an active participant on an absolutely equal footing." [13]

The latest five-year agreement was signed in August, 1970, by Secretary Rogers and Gregorio Lopez Bravo, Foreign Minister of Spain. It is a broad-gauged "Agreement of Friendship and Cooperation" covering educational, scientific, and cultural exchanges as well as mutual aid in defense. In return for continued use of the bases in Spain the United States promised "to support Spanish defense efforts, as necessary and appropriate, by contributing to the modernization of Spanish defense industries, as well as granting military assistance to Spain," subject to the appropriation of funds by Congress. It was agreed that in case of "external threat or attack against the security of the West" the two governments would consult as to when and how the United States might use the bases. In deference to the Senate, the Rusk-Castiella declaration of 1963 was dropped. As officially interpreted, the 1970 agreement contains no defense commitment to Spain, but troublesome questions remain as to whether the mere

[13] *Washington Post,* June 21, 1969, p. A2.

presence of 10,000 Americans in uniform in Spain may lead to unfortunate consequences and whether the United States has paid too much for the military convenience these bases afford.

In passing it is worthy of note that the Senate was not willing to take the State Department at its word that the new agreement involved no defense commitment. Just to make doubly sure, the Senate passed a resolution introduced by Senator Church to the effect that nothing in the agreement "should be construed as a national commitment by the United States to defend Spain." Perhaps the Senate was closing the door after the horse had been stolen. But at least it put the Senate on record as trying to limit the power of the executive to act alone in these matters.

One obvious purpose of the agreement was to draw Spain closer to the NATO family. Article 35 provides: "Both Governments consider it necessary and appropriate that the cooperation for defense regulated by this Chapter form a part of the security arrangements for the Atlantic and Mediterranean areas, and to that end they will endeavor to work out by common accord the liaison deemed advisable with the security arrangements for those areas." [14] The provision was immediately interpreted as an American coup to sneak Spain into NATO by the back door. On his return to Madrid from Washington after the signing ceremonies, Foreign Minister Bravo acknowledged that "the agreement brings us closer to NATO." [15] In a briefing on the agreement Under Secretary of State Johnson was asked if Article 35 "ties this into NATO insofar as taking into account the regional defense arrangements?" Mr. Johnson replied: "That is right. Neither one of us can be blind to that." [16] One of the specific links con-

[14] Department of State press release No. 231, August 6, 1970, p. 8.
[15] Richard Mowrer in the *Christian Science Monitor*, August 18, 1970, p. 3.
[16] Spanish Base Agreement, p. 32.

templated is the joining of the new U.S.–Spanish automated alert and control network to the aerial security system for the continent. Technical liaison arrangements are also being sought with the NATO commands in the Mediterranean and Atlantic areas.

From the military viewpoint it is wholly logical, of course, to include Spain in the defense system for Western Europe. But some of the NATO countries, notably Norway and Denmark, remain hostile to the idea of making common cause with the Franco regime. If bases in Spain and Spanish cooperation are really essential to the security of Europe, the European countries themselves should be first to recognize it. The fact that they continue to exclude the Franco government from their counsels, while the United States tries to defeat that policy by means of a bilateral arrangement, puts a strain on NATO that may outweigh any military advantage accruing from the bases in Spain. It is not the manifest destiny of the United States to force Franco down the European throat.

One other serious question about the agreement is whether it has jeopardized our long-range relations with Spain. The Franco regime cannot last forever, as the generalissimo's choice of a successor has tacitly acknowledged. If his passing from the scene should ultimately lead to a restoration of popular government in Spain, the United States will be in danger of losing not only the bases, but also the prospect of establishing friendly relations with the new Spain which would then doubtless be welcomed into NATO. Whether or not they have good reason for doing so, many Spaniards are reported to believe that the American base deal with Franco saved his regime from collapse in 1953 and kept him in power far beyond his time. As they see it, Franco is drawing upon American military might to suppress any domestic elements which may threaten his dictatorship. If this younger element comes to power any time in the near future, the Franco tarnish on the American image is not likely to wash easily.

All these factors were shunted aside, however, when the showdown on renewal of the agreement came. The administration seemed to base its decision primarily upon short-range military expediency. In defending the agreement before the Senate Foreign Relations Committee, Under Secretary of State Johnson said that the bases in Spain continue to be important in " (a) maintaining our general deterrent posture in the Mediterranean area, (b) providing the infrastructure to support our forces deployed in Europe and the Mediterranean, and (c) *contributing to our world-wide strategic and tactical mobility*" [17] (italics supplied). It is impossible to avoid the conclusion that this relation of the bases to our world policing role was in the beginning, and now remains, the dominant reason for this highly risky liaison.

In the eyes of the military the bases in Spain are essential to our security. But security in this frame of reference does not mean the protection of American territory from attack or even defense of our allies. NATO generals acknowledge that there are numerous bases between Portugal and Turkey to which the American aircraft in Spain could be transferred if necessary. The Rota harbor is not the only place from which Polaris submarines may be properly supported. The Pentagon insists on maintaining bases in Spain, despite the heavy cost in terms of misunderstanding, lost prestige, and possible military involvements, because those bases help to round out a global network of military power.

Here is the nub of the controversy, and it is disturbing to see the military have its way over powerful opposition in both Congress and the country. If the outcome may be regarded as symptomatic, the much-touted retreat from globalism still has a long way to go.

[17] Spanish Base Agreement, p. 11.

IX

The NATO Keystone

THE NORTH ATLANTIC TREATY has been the keystone of our international defense system since World War II, and it is likely to remain so. In many respects it is a unique organization. It has demonstrated the weaknesses as well as the strengths of an extended and diversified alliance, but the very fact that such a concert of powers is in its third decade of successful operation gives it a rare distinction. Never before in recorded history have fifteen countries stretched across two continents stood together for their common defense for so long a period.

The fact that NATO has never had to test its military strength in battle tends to obscure its accomplishments. No doubt it would be better known and perhaps more highly respected if it had suffered a bloodbath. Conflict and war are always more spectacular than uneasy peace. An organization that is able to ride through a turbulent era without having to meet the violent confrontation that loomed threateningly at the time of its creation may well be taken for granted. Its operations may be regarded as humdrum, and even the menace that called it into being is likely to seem somewhat unreal with the passing of time. Yet any honest appraisal must make allowance for what the world might be like without an alliance of the free nations of the west standing against tyranny, subversion, and the spread of Communism by violence within their living space. To say the very least, NATO has been sufficiently effective in dispersing the war clouds that have traditionally hung over Europe and in discouraging an East-West showdown to merit the hearty thanks of free men everywhere.

It follows that we have much to learn from NATO as a new decade unfolds. NATO reflects the best of our postwar experience in the grim business of staying alive in the nuclear age and in seeking a more stable international atmosphere. It is not tainted by any aggressive or irresponsible act. Despite the screaming from behind the Iron Curtain about hostile intentions on the part of the NATO powers, it has held rigorously to its defensive posture. Since the Council met in New York in September, 1950, to discuss protection of the NATO area against aggression of the type that had broken out in Korea, its mission has remained consistent despite the rapid evolution in international relations. This ability to cling to a moderate defensive role in the face of frequent provocation was an enormous advantage to NATO in its first two decades, and it continues to be so in the period when (hopefully) its major task may become one of the building bridges between the East and the West.

NATO's defensive role did not lead to a static policy. At the outset the organization brought into being the North Atlantic Council in addition to elaborate military commands. In 1951 the Council, meeting in Ottawa, decided to invite Greece and Turkey to join the alliance, and its membership was increased to fourteen. In 1955 the Federal German Republic became the fifteenth member; the United States and Britain agreed to maintain substantial forces on the continent of Europe; and a unified military command was established under the Supreme Allied Commander, Europe.

The response of the Soviet Union was to denounce its treaties with Britain and France and to conclude a mutual defense arrangement (the Warsaw Pact) with its satellites in Eastern Europe.

It cannot be properly said, however, that one organization merely offsets the other. The Warsaw Pact did little to change the relations between Moscow and Eastern Europe, which was already under Soviet domination. On the contrary, all the NATO countries remained independent sovereignties brought together for a common purpose without dictation or compulsion from any one of them. Such an organization, deemed essential to the survival of each member, could not allow itself to be intimidated or deterred by any tightening of Moscow's lines of control on the other side.

If NATO has made any grave mistake, it lies in not going further than it has to date in developing the political and economic ties that bind its members together. Some hopeful steps in the direction of greater cohesiveness have been taken. In 1956 a committee of three foreign ministers — Dr. Gaetano Martino of Italy, Mr. Halvard Lange of Norway, and Mr. Lester B. Pearson of Canada, the so-called "Three Wise Men" — recommended a convergence of political, economic, and cultural interests. "An Alliance in which the members ignore each other's interests, or engage in political or economic conflict, or harbour suspicions of each other," these advisers concluded, "cannot be effective either for deterrence or defence." [1] The committee expressed a widespread hope that the civil side of the alliance could be developed along with its military cooperation. The response to the challenge of the Three Wise Men has been mostly in the form of words. Aspirations easily outrun performance in this area. Yet the basic mechanism for more extensive collaboration exists, and

[1] *NATO Facts and Figures,* NATO Information Service, Brussels, 1969, p. 304.

statesmen are still grappling with ways and means of making it more useful.

The relative success of NATO is the more impressive because of the continued weakness of the United Nations. It is reasonable to assume that the Atlantic Alliance would never have come into being if the UN had been able to function as its founders intended. World War II had intensified the almost universal desire for peace to be maintained by means of international commitments against aggression. The United Nations was to have a Military Staff Committee and international forces assigned to it by all its members. But these hoped-for peace-keeping forces never came into being because of the fears of the Soviet Union that they would be used against her schemes for extending Communism by force and subversion. The USSR had already annexed all or part of eight countries with 24 million people between 1940 and 1945 and had extended her control over Poland, Czechoslovakia, Hungary, Rumania, Bulgaria, Albania, and the Soviet Zone of Germany between 1945 and 1948. This communized buffer zone contained nearly 92 million inhabitants. When it became clear that the United Nations could not be used effectively to halt the outward push of aggressive Communism, because of the permanent-power veto in the Security Council, the free nations of the western world had to fill the breach or risk a series of wars and revolutions aimed at their extinction.

It was apparent from the beginning that NATO was pinch-hitting for the paralyzed world organization. The treaty was built within the framework of the United Nations Charter. The aims of the two are virtually identical within the area where the alliance operates. The North Atlantic Treaty expresses only the right of its members to defend themselves collectively — a right specifically reserved to them by Article 51 of the United Nations Charter. The Atlantic partners further agreed to report to the Security Council any defensive action taken under the treaty and to terminate such action whenever the Security Council had taken the necessary measures to restore the peace.

With this background, NATO could cheerfully fold up whenever the United Nations might come into its own as a guarantor of international peace. Or it could logically give way, at least in theory, to any other viable grouping of nations with a better chance of saving the Atlantic community from the horrors of war in the nuclear age. But this is only another way of saying that NATO is an expedient and not necessarily a definitive end in and of itself. It has a built-in transient quality, and yet that very characteristic that made it a powerful instrument in the 1950s and 1960s continues to sustain it in the 1970s.

Realism demands that all the possibilities for supplanting NATO be viewed in proper perspective. As a practical matter, there seems to be nothing on the horizon at this time to suggest that the United Nations can be converted into a potent and reliable peace-keeping agency within the present generation so far as conflicts between the major powers are concerned. This has been acknowledged by Ambassador Charles W. Yost, former United States representative in the United Nations. In discussing ways of making the United Nations Charter more effective, he said: ". . . even if we reinvigorate UN peacekeeping to this extent, we will still be very far from enabling the United Nations to prevent threats to or breaches of the peace. Its great weakness is that it cannot enforce its decisions." [2]

Nor is there any sound basis for the assumption that the Soviet Union, despite internal weakness and the breakup of the Marxian monolith, will give up its propensity for fishing

[2] Ambassador Yost's speech to World Federalists USA, Philadelphia, February 5, 1970; Press Release USUN-13 (70).

in troubled waters wherever and whenever it sees opportunity to advance the cause of international Communism. Consequently there seems to be no possibility of changing the format of NATO so that it would be acceptable to the Soviet Union without destroying its usefulness from the viewpoint of the western democracies.

By the same token, the North Atlantic powers could not conceivably join the Warsaw Pact or anything resembling it. The Soviet invasion of Czechoslovakia in 1968 and the subsequent enunciation of the Brezhnev Doctrine — that Moscow has a right to put down any deviation from Marxism-Leninism by a country deemed to be within the "Socialist Commonwealth" — should be sufficient to indicate how far the two groups of powers are from common ground. The best that may be expected in the foreseeable future is an easing of tensions between them, possibly some progress toward limitation of nuclear weapons, and reduction of troops in the potential areas of confrontation. Initiatives in these directions are of enormous importance, and the NATO powers, with their greater basic strength, may well take the lead and go as far as prudence dictates. But whether such ventures succeed or fail or continue to be dragged out in endless profusion, the need for NATO or something comparable to it will continue. The advantages of confronting the Communist bloc by a formidable group of powers united in the determination to preserve their freedom have been amply demonstrated. It seems highly probable, therefore, that NATO will be with us for some decades to come.

For this reason the weaknesses of NATO demand no less attention than its basic strength and its achievements. NATO has experienced many of the misunderstandings, divergencies, and schisms that afflict any association of independent powers. Despite their many common interests, these countries are still set apart by history, geography, culture, political institutions, economic resources, and (in many instances) language. Merely to name them — Belgium, Canada, Denmark, France, West Germany, Greece, Iceland, Italy, Luxembourg, the Netherlands, Norway, Portugal, Turkey, the United Kingdom, and the United States — is to conjure up a multitude of conflicting interests, ideas, and traditions. In the light of history the surprising thing is not that they have sometimes pulled in different directions and left many problems unresolved but that they have clung together in their general objective of mutual protection.

Probably the most serious schism came with the dropout of France as an active partner in the defensive operations. Swayed by President de Gaulle's preoccupation with nationalism, the government at Paris gave notice in March, 1966, that it would withdraw all French forces from the international commands, wind up its representation in the NATO integrated military superstructure, and request the transfer of the International Headquarters as well as the allied units and bases then on French soil. The decision was a severe blow to the concept of collective defense, but it was far from being fatal to NATO. The remaining fourteen partners sensibly met together and then negotiated amicably with France for effectuation of the required changes. The NATO headquarters were shifted to Belgium, and SHAPE (Supreme Headquarters Allied Powers Europe) was provided with better communications systems and operation centers than it had in France. Italy was invited to provide a new home for the NATO Defense College.

France's defection left a big hole in the system and complicated the problem of defense planning in Western Europe. Undoubtedly it gave some comfort to the Kremlin and the governments of other Warsaw Pact powers. But it also demonstrated an advanced degree of sophistication in the NATO organization. There was no attempt to expel France in a fit of pique. Nor was there any disposition on the part of the other NATO powers to follow the French example. The quiet acceptance of the French decision later stood out in striking contrast to the Soviet invasion of Czechoslovakia when that unhappy country began to make some independent decisions that displeased the Communist overlords in Moscow. France is still a free and independent member of NATO. This point was underlined when Foreign Minister Michel Debré visited Washington in April, 1969, to attend a NATO ministerial meeting. His presence for the twentieth anniversary of the alliance, he said, was proof that NATO had not lost its raison d'être in French eyes. France continued to maintain military liaison with some NATO commands, to join occasionally in naval maneuvers, to participate in NATO's air defense, and to take an active part in the council's political discussions and decisions. If a showdown should come between NATO and the Warsaw Pact countries, the French are likely to be found standing beside their allies in a common defense effort. The underlying interests that hold them within the alliance are as real and as inextinguishable as they ever were.

Meanwhile NATO has won substantial prestige from following the right course in trying circumstances. An alliance dedicated to freedom, independence, and self-determination for every sovereign power could not throw those principles to the winds when a break in its ranks was threatened. It may be a negative kind of distinction that an organization achieves from an experience of this kind, but in the end its maturity of judgment may well enhance the respect for it both from within and from without. Under stress, NATO adhered to its principles. At least in the kind of world that the alliance is trying to save this is a sign of psychological and moral strength that may well offset the loss in terms of immediate military cooperation.

A more serious source of weakness has been the unwillingness of most of the partners to maintain sufficient conventional military strength to provide a reliable shield without the use of nuclear weapons. Democracies always seem to be on the short end of military power in peacetime. The history of NATO has been one of repeated fixing of military goals that have not been met. After Nikita S. Khrushchev renewed his threat to conclude a separate peace with East Germany and thus cut off the Western powers' access to Berlin, there was some improvement in the military contributions to NATO. But resolution waned as tensions were relaxed. NATO continued to be, as Hanson W. Baldwin has pointed out, "far too much form and too little substance." [3]

Although no country can escape a share of the blame for this situation, the chief deficiencies are readily traceable to the European members. They are well aware of their vulnerability to Communist subversion and possible invasion if a strong collective defensive posture is not maintained. Military authorities consistently rate the Warsaw Pact powers "vastly superior" to NATO in terms of conventional weapons. Yet the democracies of Western Europe, which are on the front line of danger, have been content to leave a disproportionate share of the defense effort to the United States. This is what one would expect in the immediate postwar days when Europe was almost bankrupt and the danger was acute. But in the subsequent years of prosperity there has been much less excuse for the continued reliance of the European partners upon American conventional forces.

In the first year of NATO (1949) the percentage of Gross National Product contributed to defense was precisely the same for the NATO countries of Europe as a whole as for the United States. It stood in both instances at 5.7 per cent. By 1952, however, the United States defense expenditures had mounted to 14.9 per cent of GNP, partly because of the war

[3] *Reader's Digest,* April, 1969, p. 161.

in Korea, compared to 8.7 per cent for the European countries as a whole. Since then the disparities have further widened. In 1967 the standing of the powers in the NATO table showing defense expenditures as a percentage of Gross National Product was as follows: Belgium, 3.3; Canada, 3.6; Denmark, 3.3; France, 6.2; West Germany, 5.3; Greece, 5.1; Italy, 3.7; Luxembourg, 1.4; Netherlands, 4.2; Norway, 4.1; Portugal, 7.4; Turkey, 5.4; United Kingdom, 6.7; United States, 10.1. The figure for the European NATO members as a whole was 5.4.[4]

Some defenders of the status quo say that the portion of a country's gross national product going into defense is not necessarily relevant to its NATO obligations. The United States devotes a relatively large portion of its output to military operations because it is a superpower with global responsibilities. What it does is not a proper criterion for judging the adequacy of the defense outlays of, say, Belgium or Norway. While there may be some validity to this argument, it can just as readily be turned around the other way: because the United States assumes obligations for the defense of freedom and independence over a very broad area, the affluent powers of Europe could fairly take over a larger part of the defense load in that part of the world where they are directly concerned. It is widely conceded that some of the less affluent NATO powers, notably Turkey and Greece, are already making substantial contributions in comparison to their resources.

The population of the NATO countries in Europe was 301,039,000 in 1967 compared to 199,118,000 for the United States. The six Common Market countries and Britain, taken together, have more potential military manpower and a larger economic output than the Soviet Union. Since Western Europe has no nuclear arsenal of its own that would put

[4] *NATO Facts and Figures,* NATO Information Service, Brussels, 1969, p. 227.

it in the military league of the superpowers, it is not in a
position to go it alone in the age of balanced terror. But,
with its command of industrial and political resources —
greater than those of any geographical unit other than the
United States — European NATO could support a much
greater conventional defense effort than it achieved in the
fifties and sixties.

Fortunately, this fact has been recognized by some European statesmen. Denis Healey, the British Defense Minister,
told a meeting of NATO parliamentarians in Washington in
October, 1969, that the European members should take over
"a fairer share" of the common defense burden.[5] In a speech
to the same assembly, NATO's Secretary General, Manlio
Brosio, also called attention to the feeling that after having
regained their economic strength, the Europeans are not
shouldering a fair share of the common effort.[6] The Canadian
Prime Minister, Pierre Trudeau, made a similar point when
he announced a phased reduction in Canada's forces in Europe in April, 1969. Without aiming any blow at NATO as
such, he said:

> NATO itself is continuously reassessing the role it plays in
> the light of changing world conditions. Perhaps the major
> development affecting NATO in Europe since the organization
> was founded is the magnificent recovery of the economic
> strength of Western Europe. There has been a very great
> change in the ability of European countries themselves to pro-
> vide necessary conventional defense forces and armaments to
> be deployed by the alliance in Europe.[7]

Incidentally, the argument would have had more force if
Canada herself had been a major contributor to NATO. Unfortunately, however, Canada had allowed her defense ex-

[5] *Washington Post*, October 22, 1969, p. A22.
[6] NATO Letter, December, 1969, NATO Information Service, Brussels.
[7] Reproduced in the *Congressional Record*, December 1, 1969, p. S15163.

penditures to shrink from 9 per cent of GNP in 1953 to 3.6 in 1967.

For several years Majority Leader Mike Mansfield of the United States Senate argued the case for trimming the American contingents in NATO. In 1969 he conceded that the time was not ripe to press his demand because of the Soviet Union's renewed occupation of Czechoslovakia. But his resolution designed to put the Senate on record for a substantial reduction in the United States' military presence in Europe came to the fore again in 1970 and 1971 with a good deal of steam behind it. The majority leader of the Senate is not a foe of NATO, nor does he wish to have all the American forces stationed in Europe come home. "Our vital interest in what transpires in Europe remains," he told his colleagues in reintroducing his resolution, "and a U.S. presence should remain." [8] He insisted, however, that a smaller force would adequately serve the purpose of a common defense. At one point in the argument he urged that the United States remove two of its five to six divisions.[9]

Mansfield's arguments were persuasive in their own setting. Looking primarily at the foreign exchange gap with Germany, which was running at about $965 million per annum at the end of 1969, he complained that the maintenance of excessive forces in Europe was a heavy drain on our resources, a source of inflation, and a factor in the reduction of the international strength of the dollar. In the second place, he contended that overparticipation by the United States in the defense of Europe had discouraged efforts on the part of our allies to develop their own capacity to stand up against potential aggression.

From the eastern side of the Atlantic, however, any proposed sudden reduction of American forces in Europe takes

[8] Ibid., p. S15164.
[9] *Washington Post*, January 21, 1970, p. A10.

on a somewhat different appearance. Probably the biggest hurdle that NATO had to clear in its first two decades was the skepticism of Europeans that Washington would risk a nuclear war to save Germany, Norway, and other northern members of the alliance from possible Soviet invasion. The presence of a substantial body of Americans in uniform in Germany stood as a sort of physical guarantee that the United States would be involved in any outbreak of hostilities from the beginning, and that consequently the pledge that an attack upon one would be treated as an attack upon all would stand up under fire. A sudden weakening of American forces actually present on the Continent would undoubtedly be interpreted as a cooling of Washington toward this NATO commitment.

If the State Department should find some way of reassuring our European allies on this point, moreover, it is feared that they would interpret any sudden cutback of American forces in NATO as a signal that the dangers that called the alliance into being had passed. The Nixon administration is fearful that compliance with the Mansfield resolution, instead of providing impetus for Western Europe to build up its armed forces, would give an excuse for the European allies to order a comparable trimming. The issue is, therefore, fraught with delicacy and needs to be approached with more concern for the future of NATO than for easing the United States' balance-of-payments problem and reducing the NATO drain on the U.S. budget.

Some curtailment of the American forces in NATO was brought about without fanfare in 1968 and 1969. At the end of 1967 about 372,000 Americans in uniform were in Europe, including the personnel of the 6th Fleet in the Mediterranean, the troops assigned to Turkey, and those manning the military bases in Spain. With them were 240,000 dependents, a total of 612,000. Two years later this total had shrunk to

about 550,000, composed of 315,000 men in the services, 235,-
000 dependents and 14,000 civilians employed by the United
States Government. This is a fairly substantial curtailment,
and it suggests a way in which the needed adjustment can be
brought about without any dramatic gesture that would lend
itself to misinterpretation.

Another means of distributing the burden more evenly
would be for the European countries to share or take over
some of the direct costs of maintaining American troops on
their soil. The usual pattern, in NATO and elsewhere, has
been for the United States to build bases in the country to
be defended even though those bases were for joint use of the
two countries and American troops could not take them
along on their ultimate departure. But this practice became
increasingly dubious. In December, 1970, the ten "Eurogroup" members of NATO agreed at Brussels to finance certain improvements so that they could be completed in five
years instead of ten, as originally planned. Included in the
projects are improved electronic communications between
the member countries and "hardened" shelters for NATO
aircraft, estimated to cost a total of $420 million. A second
part of the agreement called for the contribution of new
planes and other weapons to NATO. Skeptics expressed fear
that the agreement would not be carried out in full measure,
but President Nixon was sufficiently impressed by it to pledge
that the American contribution to NATO would not be
diluted.

It may reasonably be argued that the European members of
NATO did not go so far as they should have gone to balance
the defense burden, although the program approved at Brussels could involve the expenditure of nearly a billion dollars
over the next five years. At least it is obvious that Congress
could not now sharply trim the United States' contribution
to NATO without dealing it a critical blow. The step-up of

the European effort was made specifically contingent upon the maintenance of the American forces in Europe "at substantially current levels." Europe responded, at least in some measure, to the Nixon Doctrine, which called upon other developed nations "to assume greater responsibility for leadership and initiative in the affairs of the major regions of the world," [10] especially in the framework of regional organizations. If no east-west agreement can be reached on the mutual reduction of forces, it may be necessary to ask the "Eurogroup" to do more, but this is a very different matter from a backward step in Washington that would undercut NATO. The NATO bridge across the Atlantic should not be sacrificed under any circumstances.

With the opening of a new era of negotiations with the Soviet Union, strong hope persisted for an agreement that would involve troop reductions on both sides of the east-west line of confrontation. To say the least, that hope could not be strengthened by a conspicuous, unilateral trimming on the NATO side in advance of, or during, the negotiations. The cut-back-now forces are very impatient with this line of reasoning. Some excuse for delay can always be found, they say, but this raises the question of what is the central purpose of the United States' participation in NATO. If the dominant aim is to buttress the safeguards to peace by maintaining an alert and healthy alliance with the free and democratic peoples of Western Europe, then the accomplishment of secondary aims must be brought about by means that will not risk its dissolution.

In the background is a more profound reason for caution and diplomacy. Suppose official Washington should say to the powers of Western Europe, "We intend to bring a large part of our NATO forces home, and if you want to match the

[10] Secretary William P. Rogers' address to the Conference for Editors and Broadcasters, January 15, 1970.

Soviet military on the other side of the line you will have to supply the necessary conventional strength yourselves." The effect of any such blunt ultimatum might be to compromise our own security. It is all too obvious that if NATO should allow its conventional forces to dwindle to a point where they could offer little resistance to a Soviet attack, the only security behind western civilization would be nuclear power. In such circumstances NATO would be forced to use tactical nuclear weapons very early in any armed clash that might develop. Russia could be expected to respond with more deadly "nukes," and it could be a matter of only days or even hours before the arsenals of intercontinental ballistic missiles would be unloosed, with the potential of destroying the world.

Hope of avoiding this kind of holocaust has been the strongest factor in keeping substantial American forces in Europe in recent years. It still provides a powerful incentive for a large-enough-to-be-convincing United States contribution to the conventional shield. In this era when a single nation or continent on fire may quickly touch off a worldwide conflagration every country has an interest in aiding the fire wagon at the most incendiary points. The United States cannot afford to risk a nuclear confrontation every time a crisis may arise in Berlin or elsewhere on the Continent any more than the European partners can. Of course this does not mean that unequal sacrifices for common benefits can be safely ignored. NATO is likely to be needed for the long pull as well as for the short pull, and disparities of this kind sow the seeds of disintegration. They should not be allowed to continue any longer than is necessary for an orderly and amicable adjustment, but the manner in which such actions are sought remains crucial.

History, geography, technology, and a thousand other forces have combined to give the United States the only formidable nuclear arsenal in the west. Whether or not this is distasteful to our NATO partners, it is a fact that cannot be readily changed. Some of the European members of NATO have signed the nuclear nonproliferation treaty designed to prevent the spread of the ultimate weapon to countries that do not now have it. Western Europe has in fact forsworn the bomb. Security for that continent seems to lie in a firm attachment to the American nuclear shield, while maintaining enough conventional military strength to make resort to nuclear defense highly improbable. If the United States carries out its primary mission and also provides the tactical nuclear bombs to back up conventional weapons in case of necessity on the battlefields of Europe, clearly the other members of NATO can be reasonably asked to supply most of the conventional forces needed in the buffer areas.

There are many who would like to see Western Europe develop a convincing defense capacity of its own wholly independent of the United States. No doubt that course would have some advantages in an age without nuclear power. In the real world of the 1970s, however, the shattering potential of the hydrogen bomb overshadows all other force that may be assembled. At least for the foreseeable future, security for Western Europe must be linked to the American nuclear shield. France has not demonstrated capacity to rival the superpowers. Britain lacks the resources for such a role. It is estimated that West Germany could produce nuclear bombs within a year,[11] but she is forbidden by treaty to do so. The bomb in the hands of the Bonn government would be more conducive to war than to peace. In the light of twentieth-century history, German H-bombs would be regarded as unthinkable by the allies and irrational by the Germans themselves. The merger of German security with the security of Western Europe is an achievement that must not be sacrificed,

[11] Hanson W. Baldwin in *Reader's Digest*, April, 1969, p. 168.

and the best means of retaining it is the maintenance of a vigorous NATO functioning in close partnership with American nuclear power. Even if we could assume that the Soviet menace that brought NATO into being will fade into history during the decades ahead, the preservation of a strong North Atlantic Alliance would still be highly desirable as a means of retaining this coordination of Western European forces.

Development of an acceptable relationship between the non-nuclear powers with the one superpower in the alliance has been a baffling problem. In 1962 the United States renewed its pledge that it would make available to the alliance the nuclear weapons for its defense and discuss the conditions under which nuclear weapons should be used. While this was gratifying to the Europeans in one respect, it left them with the feeling of having little to say on the basic questions of their security. Would the United States risk New York or Washington to defend Berlin? After the Soviet Union acquired a large stock of nuclear bombs and the means of delivering them, there was substantial skepticism on the Continent as to whether the American pledge could be trusted if the flames of conflict should happen to be confined to Europe. President John F. Kennedy and Prime Minister Harold Macmillan wrestled with this problem in 1962 and came up with a plan to create a NATO multilateral nuclear force to which submarines armed with Polaris missiles would be assigned. They also proposed commitment of parts of the American and British nuclear forces to NATO. At the meeting of NATO ministers in Ottawa in May, 1963, however, these proposed experiments simmered down to the naming of a SACEUR staff deputy responsible for nuclear affairs, the assignment of the United Kingdom's v-bomber force and three United States Polaris submarines to SACEUR, and some broader participation of European officers in NATO's nuclear planning and activities.

In 1966 the NATO Council set up the Nuclear Defense Affairs Committee and a seven-member Nuclear Planning Group. NATO officials described the agreement at that time as providing for "a flexible and balanced range of responses, conventional and nuclear, to all levels of aggression or threats of aggression." [12] The task of the committees was to determine under what circumstances the large stockpile of United States tactical nuclear weapons now in Europe would be used. In theory, the policy devised is a relatively simple one. It contemplates that, in the event of Soviet aggression against any NATO country, the allies would defend themselves with conventional forces so long as possible, then use tactical nuclear weapons to supplement their conventional defenses, and as a last resort strike directly at the USSR with intercontinental ballistic missiles. In practice, however, application of the policy under the stress of a civilization-imperiling emergency might prove to be extremely difficult. The one thing clear at present is that the options open to NATO would be dangerously narrowed by failure to maintain enough conventional firepower to deter any reckless Soviet adventures not intended to provoke a nuclear confrontation.

Opinions differ widely as to how adequate the NATO forces were at the beginning of the decade. One officer is quoted as saying that the period during which NATO's conventional forces could stand up against a Soviet attack would be "very damn short." [13] Gloomy military spokesmen are likely to estimate the superiority of the Warsaw Pact forces to the NATO forces at any point from two to one to five to one. They are especially worried by the fact that the Soviets maintain some armored divisions for which unarmored NATO troops would be no match. Soviet fighting planes are said to be not only more numerous but also more modern than NATO's. Beginning in 1969, moreover, the rapidly mount-

[12] *NATO Facts and Figures,* NATO Information Service, Brussels, 1969, p. 59.
[13] Quoted by Hanson W. Baldwin in *Reader's Digest,* April, 1969, p. 168.

ing Soviet fleet in the Mediterranean became a source of increasing worry. In the face of all this, however, experts in the State Department insist that the disparity between the Warsaw Pact and NATO strength is not great. It is admitted that many NATO divisions need new equipment, better logistical support, and additional recruits to fill up their ranks. Some improvements were in the works in 1970 among the European contingents, but it seems highly improbable that the gap between the forces immediately available in NATO and those in Eastern Europe will be closed. The best that can be anticipated is that drastic, symbolical slashes will be avoided and that NATO can evolve into its prospective new role without premature or excessive emasculation on the military side.

No doubt the major reason for confidence on the diplomatic side as to the adequacy of NATO's 1970 posture, in contrast to the fears of the military, was the more relaxed attitude that seems to prevail in Moscow. Official Washington was convinced that the Soviet Union did not want a clash with the United States under conditions then prevailing. Moscow was preoccupied by her disputes and border clashes with Red China and her attempt to hold Czechoslovakia and other satellites of Eastern Europe in the so-called Socialist Commonwealth. No less sobering from the Soviet viewpoint was the failure of that country to achieve the industrial miracles that were talked about so much a few years ago. The Russians were no longer bellowing threats that they would bury the United States, as Khrushchev did in his day. As the new decade began they were conscious of the fact that the United States had a gross national product more than twice their own. So the time seemed ripe for negotiations with the Americans instead of moving toward an armed confrontation.

Whether or not this was a correct reading of the Moscow mood, it coincided with the Nixon-Rogers thesis that the

United States must take risks — calculated risks, not foolish risks — for the attainment of peace. One of those risks was the acceptance of a somewhat inferior status for NATO while seeking to negotiate limitations on nuclear weapons and a balanced reduction of forces. Hope for the achievement of major objectives through these negotiations remained extremely limited, but any weighing of the relative risks in the scales of current realities seemed to come out heavily in favor of the conciliatory approach.

NATO may well have a great future, but it is more likely to be a future in negotiations for peace than merely in the maintenance of military prowess. In the 1950s and 1960s NATO demonstrated that it could prevent the shaping of Europe's future by hostile military forces. Its task for the 1970s is to heal the wounds remaining from World War II and the subsequent cold war, and that may well require a greater degree of cohesiveness than its successful defensive posture of the past.

President Nixon sought to push NATO in this direction when he addressed the foreign ministers of the alliance on its twentieth anniversary. "The allies have learned to concert their military forces," he said. "Now, in the light of the vast military, economic and political changes of two decades, we must devise better means of harmonizing our policies . . . By its nature, ours is more than a military alliance; and the time has come to turn a part of our attention to those non-military areas in which we all could benefit from increased collaboration." [14] The President asked that the deputy foreign ministers meet periodically "for a high-level review of major long-range problems before the alliance"; that a special political planning group be set up for continuous study of "longer-range problems"; and that a "social dimension" be added "to deal with our concern for the quality of life in this

[14] *New York Times*, April 11, 1969, p. C14.

final third of the 20th century." The President's effort to internationalize his campaign for an improved environment seemed to be going rather far afield, but his speech was followed by an intensification of political activity in NATO.

Without trying to penetrate too far into the future, it does appear that NATO has an enormous potential for useful service in the post-cold-war era. It is the strongest international force in the world working for peace in a traditional background of freedom and economic progress. Though it is estimated to cost the United States between $13 billion and $15 billion a year, it is worth the price. Efforts will undoubtedly continue to induce the European partners to pay a fairer share of the total burden, but this is a relatively minor problem. The overriding consideration is that the alliance retain its vitality and its capacity to evolve with the changing time. It would be a tragedy not only for western civilization but for all mankind if this experiment in collective security, in behalf of people who wish to live and let live, were to falter.

A virile NATO organization is not antagonistic to the concept of a more closely united Europe. Washington officials were wholly sincere (although somewhat naive and over-eager) when they sponsored a European Defense Community some years ago. They have been consistent in their support of the Common Market in Western Europe. When the unity movement on the Continent has been carried to its utmost bounds of feasibility, however, there will still be need for close collaboration with the transplanted Europeans on the western side of the Atlantic. The peoples of the North Atlantic basin probably have more in common than the peoples of any other comparable area unless it be the vast land mass of the Soviet Union. The peace of the world through many future decades may depend upon their ability to cling together, despite numerous differences and conflicting interests, for the one supreme task of preserving their civilization.

NATO emerges, therefore, as a prime necessity of the fore-seeable future. It remains a keystone of inestimable impor-tance in American foreign policy. If similar conditions pre-vailed in other parts of the world, it would be a useful model that could be reproduced elsewhere. Unfortunately, there are no parallel conditions in Asia, Africa, or even Latin America. But this does not diminish the significance of a policy that is right for the area in which it is successfully functioning. The maintenance of NATO and its adjustment to the newer tasks that are evolving in the Atlantic and the Mediterranean basins will doubtless be one of the greatest responsibilities of American statesmanship for many years to come.

X

Too Much American Presence

THE EXCESSIVE AMERICAN PRESENCE in NATO can best be seen from the perspective of Turkey. Since Turkey joined the alliance in 1952, she has been a sincere and devoted member. Of all the nations in the alliance, none is more in need of international help in maintaining its independence and integrity than Turkey or more appreciative of the help that has been given. Yet the Turks in recent years have been deeply troubled by the price they have had to pay for their security. Irritations, especially those aimed at the United States, have at times placed some rather severe strains upon the alliance.

The story of the postwar relationship between the United States and Turkey begins with the crisis of 1947. For rather obvious reasons of geography, the Soviet Union directed its severest pressures (beyond the limits of the Eastern European satellites that were already under its domination) against Turkey and Greece. Not only were there territorial claims upon Turkey's border provinces of Kars and Ardahan. Moscow also demanded bases in the Straits linking the Black Sea to the Mediterranean. Fearing that their independence was at stake, the Turks courageously resisted the threatened encroachments. When the United States offered help under the

Truman Doctrine, they eagerly embraced it and relations between the two countries became unusually warm and cordial. In the years that followed, Turkey became a major beneficiary of American aid. The volume of aid given was similar to that which went to Korea and Taiwan.

The United States was also highly pleased with the arrangement because Turkey provided valuable listening points close to the Soviet Union and military bases of great strategic value if the cold war should turn into a hot one. Turkey thus became an important participant in the policy of containing the USSR at a time when it was feared that the masters of Moscow were determined to extend their Communist system to every vulnerable nation. When Turkey later came into NATO, the new relationship was superimposed upon the Turco-American partnership that was already well advanced. Though the commitment was broadened, Turkey's contacts with NATO continued to have a predominantly American flavor.

This marriage of convenience was the more artificial because Turkey is not well known in the United States and because of the intense nationalism of the Turks. The Ottoman Empire had cultivated xenophobia for several centuries and kept the Turks in constant fear of their neighbors. When Kemal Ataturk founded the Republic of Turkey on the ruins of the empire after World War I, he sought to develop friendly relations with the west, but ingrained attitudes in regard to such basic concepts as nationalism do not change overnight. In their current pursuit of economic prosperity and military security the Turks are still highly self-reliant. It is not surprising that the continued presence of large numbers of Americans in their country, after the menace from the north had substantially diminished, should cool the enthusiasm of the Truman Doctrine era.

As the years passed, moreover, American economic and

military aid, which reached a total of $134 million in 1967, enhanced the ability of the Turks to carry their own burdens. The Americans taught them to build roads and helped them to start a modern network of highways. When the aid diminished, they continued to change the map of Turkey on their own resources. Their economic progress has been good, despite some political grumbling by the opposition, with an annual growth of gross national product ranging from 6 to 7 per cent in recent years. Their economic progressivism is perhaps best illustrated by the 1970 plans for a $75,000,000 bridge over the Bosporus and another span over the Golden Horn in Istanbul, with a modern expressway linking the two.

Domestic confidence was further enhanced by the country's handling of its internal Communist problem. The Communist Party was outlawed. Some individuals clung to Communist beliefs, but they faced insuperable difficulties because Communism in Turkey is regarded as a denial of nationalism, which is anathema to a large majority of the people. So the danger of subversion from within the country remained remote. Even the left-wing Turkish Labor Party, a haven for Communists who could not operate in the open, was reduced from fifteen to two seats in the parliamentary election of October, 1969.

Unlike some of the other NATO allies, Turkey also built up a lusty defense of her own. Though she has a population of only about 33 million and a per capita income in the neighborhood of only $300 a year, she keeps more than half a million men in her armed services. The percentage of her gross national product spent for defense (5.4 per cent) is a little less than the comparable figures for Britain and France, but substantially above the average for the smaller countries in NATO. Only the United States, the Soviet Union, China, and India have more men under arms than Turkey.

From this background it should have been obvious from

the beginning that a conspicuous American military presence in Turkey would sooner or later produce friction. The inevitable was delayed, however, until the Cyprus crisis of 1964 touched off a sort of anti-American explosion. The two eastern NATO members, Turkey and Greece, were at the brink of war in support of the clashing Turkish and Greek factions on that troubled island. The Turks reclaimed, presumably for their own contemplated military use, a base previously committed to NATO. From Washington it appeared that the whole eastern wing of NATO was about to collapse in a futile bloodbath that would undermine the whole concept of an alliance capable of settling its own differences and protecting its members against external aggression.

On June 5 President Johnson sent a stiff warning to Ismet Inönü, then Prime Minister of Turkey, after receiving information through diplomatic channels to the effect that Turkey was contemplating occupation of a portion of Cyprus by military force. The letter is said to have been written late at night by George W. Ball, then Under Secretary of State, but such messages usually pass through several hands at the State Department. In rather blunt language the letter told the Prime Minister that such a course of action would not be "consistent with the commitment of your Government to consult fully in advance with us." Treating the issue as one of war or peace, the letter stated: "I put to you personally whether you really believe that it is appropriate for your Government, in effect, to present a unilateral decision of such consequence to an ally who has demonstrated such staunch support over the years as has the United States for Turkey." In conclusion the President added a virtual ultimatum:

I must, therefore, inform you in the deepest friendship that unless I can have your assurance that you will not take such action without further and fullest consultation I cannot accept your injunction to Ambassador Hare of secrecy and must immediately ask for emergency meetings of the NATO Council and the United Nations Security Council.[1]

The Turks were furious. Prime Minister Inönü bowed to the President's demand and later visited Washington to complete the consultation, but resentment ran high. Inönü was especially indignant because the President had assumed that the purpose of the Turks was to partition the island and because of the hint in Johnson's letter that the NATO allies might not rush to the aid of Turkey if Turkish intervention in Cyprus, without the consent of her allies, should lead to involvement with the Soviet Union. Inönü responded with a good deal of heat that "There could be no shadow of a doubt about the obligation to protect Turkey within the NATO Alliance" in such a situation. "If NATO's structure is so weak as to give credit to the aggressor's allegations," he wrote, "then it means that this defect of NATO needs really to be remedied." [2]

Despite the lack of diplomatic finesse in his letter, the American President probably took the only course open to him to avert a calamity for all the NATO powers. Nevertheless, the Turks, even those who understood the necessity of the President's power play, were shocked to discover that an issue of primary importance to Turkey aroused no comparable passion in Washington. To the Turkish hinterland it looked as if the arrogant superpower across the Atlantic was sacrificing a major Turkish interest to serve its own purposes.

Rumors spread to the effect that the United States 6th Fleet in the Mediterranean was interposed between Turkey and Cyprus to prevent the threatened invasion. Actually the 6th

[1] *Middle East Journal*, Summer 1966, Vol. 20 No. 3, pp. 386–393.
[2] Ibid.

Fleet was not in the vicinity for the specific reason that the United States did not wish to risk embroilment in the Greek-Turkish quarrel. Nevertheless, the rumors persisted and were echoed and reechoed by the leftist factions. There is evidence that these rumors remained a fixed staple of Turkish belief years after the crisis had subsided. Officials in Ankara knew the facts and understood the reasoning that prompted President Johnson to intervene. It was not, however, an issue on which reasoning could quiet emotions, and so the previous popularity of everything American in Turkey seemed to take a nose dive.

After this release of emotions other irritants were magnified. Turks who had been indulgent before remembered that they had been offended by the reckless driving of American soldiers stationed in their country. Americans were also associated with unreasonable pay differentials and black marketing. It was apparent too that a new generation was coming of age — young men and women who remembered little or nothing of the dark days before the Truman Doctrine and Turkey's adherence to NATO. With the advancing industrial development, new opportunities were opening and these changes seemed to encourage dissent, disorder, and challenges to the establishment. Finally, the disillusionment gave the left-wing elements new hope of driving the Americans out. Marxist socialism was flowering belatedly in some intellectual circles in Turkey at the time for the simple reason that the Turkish government had previously banned all Communist literature. When the ban was lifted with the advent of a more liberal and democratic government, some Turks found handy Communist slogans to throw at the Americans. For the most part their campaign was subtle, not seeking the destruction of NATO — an impossible goal — or even expulsion of the Yankees but serving to discredit all foreigners. Since the Americans were the only conspicuous foreigners in the country, the brunt of this xenophobia fell on them.

Relations were further worsened by furious denunciation of the United States in the Turkish press. In the eyes of Turkish editors Washington had sacrificed the fundamental interests of Turkey in order to favor Greece. It made no difference that the United States was being similarly denounced in Athens. The nature of the alliance was poorly understood by many people in Turkey, and the magnitude of the American presence contributed much to the conviction that Turkey was being exploited to serve Yankee purposes.

When the 6th Fleet visited Istanbul in the summer of 1969, students demonstrated and two United States sailors were tossed into the Bosporus. The American ambassador's car was burned during his visit to a university and a figure supposedly representing him was symbolically hanged. When negotiations between the American Air Force and a Turkish labor union broke down, there was mass picketing in violation of the law and some incidents involving strikers and Air Force personnel. At times the union cut off all access by the Air Force to its military facilities and closed the ports in Izmir, Istanbul, and Iskenderun through which supplies for the bases were shipped. One of the demands upon the Air Force was for a voice in management decisions. The dispute was finally settled by negotiations.

With such an accumulation of irritants, the State Department in Washington decided to make the American target less conspicuous in Turkey. A reduction of personnel by 1000 was announced in March, 1969, but this left about 20,000 American servicemen and their dependents still there and most of them concentrated in a few locations. The military bases at Incirlick and Cigli are relatively isolated, and no serious incidents have been reported from those areas. In Istanbul a relatively few Americans are not very noticeable among three million Turks. In Ankara, however, a serious problem remained at the end of 1970 despite the closing of a PX selling goods to Americans and a first-run movie theater operating for Americans only. The headquarters of the American military advisors was still in the center of the city where it served as a lightning rod for demonstrators, rock-throwing students, and others intent on disruption of the alliance. It would have been difficult to have designed a more inept flaunting of the U.S. presence in Turkey if a good deal of thought had been given to such an aim.

President Nixon may well have had Turkey especially in mind when he made partnership the central theme of his message to Congress on foreign policy on February 18, 1970. Referring to Europe and NATO, he said:

> We must change the pattern of American predominance, appropriate to the postwar era, to match the new circumstances of today.

Probably nowhere in the world was his statement more welcome than in Turkey, for the Turks want to be friends. They feel a strong necessity for continued cooperation with NATO, but they don't want to be pushed around, and they seem quite determined not to slip into the role of an American satellite.

Some observers feel that the post-Cyprus attitudes are a much sounder basis on which to build a satisfactory relationship than the illusory and unrealistic ties that existed before. Each country now knows the other better. Both are now freed from the pretense that they see eye to eye in all things. Perhaps this will bring greater appreciation for the area of basic interests that they do have in common. This is likely to be dependent, however, on a substantially less conspicuous American presence in Turkey. For the Turks, there is little distinction between NATO and the U.S.A. Americans have occupied the big bases that are a part of the NATO defense system. It is the Americans who have flaunted their affluence in contrast to the relative Turkish poverty. Most seriously of all, it was the American President who, in the greatest postwar crisis for Turkey, stepped in and told the government at Ankara what it must not do. It can be reasonably argued that this act of intervention from Washington was imperative for the sake of NATO, Western Europe, and even for the Turks themselves and their ethnic brethren on the island of Cyprus, who might have been slaughtered before the Turks could have arrived. But the fact remains that the burden of stopping a bloodbath within the NATO family should not have fallen almost solely upon the President of the United States.

The experience argues powerfully for a better mechanism within NATO to meet crises of this kind. The first responsibility of that collective defense system is to keep the peace among its own members, and this necessitates some orderly means of settling disputes that will inevitably arise from time to time. As President Nixon said in his 1970 foreign policy message: "We have learned to integrate our forces; we now need better means of harmonizing our policies." NATO's future will not be secure until it has found a way of adjusting differences between its members within the organization without relying upon emergency ultimatums from Washington.

In the cooler atmosphere that prevailed after the Cyprus ultimatum, Turkey's relations with the Soviet Union also underwent substantial changes. Trade between the two countries increased. Turkey was undoubtedly concerned about the developing Soviet fleet in the Mediterranean, but its response was to seek relaxation of tensions between Moscow and Ankara. The ferment in evidence at the beginning of the seventies will doubtless bring new relationships in Eastern as well as Western Europe, and this again gives special emphasis to the need for stronger policy-making machinery in NATO.

The chance for NATO to continue coasting along successfully on its laurels of the last two decades is not, therefore, very good. With Cyprus still a smoldering volcano, and with Greece a growing embarrassment, the great experiment in collective security will need all the statesmanship that can be mustered in Europe and North America to meet its challenges. No broad alliance in a dynamic age can be a static affair. Our own country evolved from a handful of scattered colonies into a transcontinental superpower, without any calamitous break in its continuity, because it has, as Chief Justice Charles Evans Hughes once said, a "marching Constitution." The North Atlantic Treaty area is not indulging in dreams of union, but it will need the capacity to march toward greater cohesiveness in the realm of collective security if it is to fulfill its promise as the world's foremost keeper of the peace.

XI

Seeds of Disintegration

THE POSITIVE ASPECTS of the NATO experiment were blurred in a most unfortunate manner in 1967 by the aberrations of Greece. The colonels who seized power in Athens gave an ironic twist to the whole concept of an association of free peoples standing together for defense of their way of life. They raised anew the question of whether an alliance of independent democracies can hold together if minority factions are free to take over a government by force and establish themselves as the arbiters of the future.

From the beginning the alliance has justified its existence by proclaiming itself a shield for human rights. Of course peace and security always loomed large as the foremost raisons d'être. But even before those basics are mentioned in the treaty its preamble declares that the parties to it "are determined to safeguard the freedom, common heritage and civilization of their peoples, founded on the principles of democracy, individual liberty and the rule of law." [1] The members were screened to assure a fundamental compatibility of their political institutions. The mesh must have been

---

[1] "Legislation on Foreign Relations With Explanatory Notes," Joint Committee print for Senate Foreign Relations and House Foreign Affairs Committees (Washington: Government Printing Office, 1968), p. 603.

coarsened somewhat to let Portugal through, but Spain with its dictatorial Franco regime did not get close to admittance. Greece and Turkey were invited to join the alliance in 1951 because it was assumed that they were strongly committed to their own versions of popular government and that they would constitute a vital eastern barrier to the spread of Communism.

In the prior postwar years Greece had demonstrated a remarkable capacity to stand up against subversion and the forces of chaos. Despite the withdrawal of British troops from Greece in the spring of 1947, that country fought courageously against the Communist forces pressing from within and without. Its determination against discouraging odds convinced President Harry S Truman that the United States should step in with substantial aid, thus giving birth to the Truman Doctrine. The gist of the American President's statement to a joint session of Congress was: "I believe that it must be the policy of the United States to support free peoples who are resisting attempted subjugation by armed minorities or by outside pressures." [2] Congress responded by appropriating $400 million for aid to Greece and Turkey and authorized the dispatch of civilian and military missions to those countries. Greece responded by cutting off the Communist infiltrations and by bringing her own lawless elements under control.

From this background it was widely assumed, when Greece was admitted to NATO a few years later, that she had a secure claim to a place in the free world. But democracy in Greece proved to be short on durability. There was, to be sure, a period of stability and considerable growth (1956–1964) under the conservative administration of Prime Minister C. Caramanlis, but criticism arose because many did not share in the growth, job opportunities were inadequate, and

[2] Harry S Truman, *Memoirs*, Vol. II (Garden City: Doubleday, 1956), p. 106.

there was a lag in educational reforms. The Caramanlis regime was succeeded by that of George Papandreou and the Center Union Party, which won an impressive victory on the basis of promises for better distribution of income, tax reform, more rapid modernization of Greece, and curtailment of the power of the King. Violent opposition soon developed, however, on the part of the crown, the armed forces, and many business leaders of the country. A flimsy "treason plot" was ascribed to the Prime Minister's son. In retaliation the Papandreou regime revived old charges of election rigging. As the conflict intensified, the elected government was overthrown. A series of improvised parliamentary governments multiplied the chaos until the Conservative and Central Union Parties agreed near the end of 1966 to hold elections and restore parliamentary government. At this point a group of fifteen or twenty military men stepped in and took over a government in a sad state of disarray.

The excuse for the coup was that Greece was once more in danger of a Communist takeover, but no substantial evidence of any such threat could be found by impartial observers. The truth appears to be that the political leaders of Greece involved themselves in such a mess that they became a pushover for a little band of adventurers pretending to save their country from chaos and corruption. Whatever support George Papadopoulos and his country-boy colonels were able to command seemed to be based on a popular belief that democracy had failed in a crucial hour.

The colonels undoubtedly thought they were rendering a great service to the Greek people. Most of them hail from the rural areas where they were nourished on the ideas that politics is dirty, that the press is corrupt, and that the universities and intellectuals are not to be trusted. With a kind of populist zeal, they set themselves the task of reforming Greek society so as to keep the evils of politics, urban centers, and big business in their places. The colonels are likely to assert that they do indeed believe in democracy, but only democracy *for* the people and not *by* the people. It follows that their methods are censorship or suppression of the press, punishment or exile of their political opponents, public works to improve living conditions, and "education" of the people so that parliamentary government will someday become feasible once more.

One of the avowed aims of the junta is to restore economic and political stability to Greece so that she may remain a faithful and useful member of NATO. From the beginning the colonels embraced the NATO slogans in a manner that has been highly embarrassing for the other members of the alliance. They seek to give the impression that the only way to protect the eastern flank of NATO is full cooperation of all members of the alliance with themselves. When such cooperation is given, even though reluctantly and on a reduced scale, it becomes in turn an argument to their propaganda-fed people that the regime is in good standing with the free world.

Opponents of the junta insist, on the contrary, that Greece's participation in NATO has been critically weakened since the coup of the colonels in April, 1967. In the first place, the critics say, the junta has decimated the armed forces by ousting an alarming number of officers deemed to be "unreliable." [3] The ax is said to have fallen with special severity on the officers opposed to the junta, many of whom had fought against the Communists in the Greek guerrilla war. Seasoned observers in Athens believe that this charge is exaggerated and that at least some of the officers were legitimately retired because of age, but if there is any truth at all in the charge the effect on officer morale may be serious.

A more subtle contention is that, in any event, Greece would be a cipher in any military showdown that might arise

[3] See article "Greece — A New Vietnam?" by Elias P. Demetracopoulos, reproduced in the *Congressional Record*, August 5, 1969, p. S9170.

because the junta has converted the army into an internal security force. The junta found it necessary to defuse the Cyprus crisis in 1967, it is said, because it could not risk full mobilization. The reasoning is that full mobilization would, in all probability, lead to overthrow of the regime and that therefore NATO cannot reasonably rely upon Greece to meet its commitments in case of necessity. Here again the danger may be exaggerated, but the risks of relying upon a regime that arouses the hostility of a vast number of its people must be taken into account.

Some NATO officials are quite properly worried by the tendency toward identification of that organization with the hated junta in the minds of the Greek people. The colonels never miss an opportunity to bask in the popularity of NATO. Apparently some Greeks and other Europeans believe that Washington had a hand in the 1967 coup, by either commission or omission, and that it then kept the colonels in power for its own purposes. While there is not a shred of evidence to this effect, the mere fact that NATO continued to work with the colonels seemed to lend credence to the rumors, with damaging psychological effects to the alliance.

There is no easy escape from this dilemma. The Johnson administration manifested its concern about the nature of the coup by withholding the delivery of some tanks, planes, and other heavy arms due Greece under previous arrangements, but it continued to send ammunition, spare parts, and so forth to avoid the impression of a complete break. Secretary of Defense Clark M. Clifford explained this policy to the Senate Foreign Relations Committee in these words: "I believe that we deal with a highly imperfect world, and if we were to confine our help to our Allies on the basis of our approving completely the different types of governments that existed then, I believe that NATO would disintegrate, and I believe that would be a calamity." [4] When the Soviet Union

4 Ibid.

invaded Czechoslovakia, the flow of American arms to Greece was increased somewhat despite the colonels' complete disregard of Washington's desire to see constitutional government restored.

The Nixon administration continued its predecessor's ambivalent policy toward Greece. For nearly a year the American Embassy in Athens was left vacant as an indication of Washington's coolness toward the regime. American observers in both capitals came to feel, however, that an ambassador would be more effective in carrying out the U.S. policy. In the absence of a civilian head of the American staff in Athens, representatives of the Pentagon had appeared to be in league with the colonels. Ambassador Henry J. Tasca, a career diplomat, finally arrived in Athens early in 1970 and began cautiously to swing policy in the other direction. About the same time, the State Department reiterated its regrets that the colonels had not permitted a restoration of constitutional government, along with its continued belief that there was little the United States could legitimately do to influence the course of events in another country. Major arms shipments to Greece were resumed in September, 1970.

The concern in Washington and other NATO capitals was accentuated by the general apathy of the Greek people. Some émigrés and their supporters carried on a furious campaign against Papadopoulos and his colonels in the late 1960s but they seemed to produce scarcely a ripple in Greece itself. Although the junta remained highly unpopular in Athens, resentment fell far short of the boiling point. There was very little evidence of oppression on the surface. People went about their business in cool disregard of the colonels and their work, as solid citizens are wont to do when there is a disgrace in the family.

One source of unrest was the continued punishment of some of the estimated 6000 former officials, legislators, military men, and others who were arrested following the coup.

Some were still awaiting trial for alleged offenses against the regime at the beginning of 1970, but the number held had dwindled to about 300 in the spring of 1971, and the regime promised to release most of these prisoners. Many Greeks were also annoyed by the junta's spy system designed to suppress opposition before it could even smolder. Certainly they were aware of the heavy hands of the colonels on the press and the schools. Many were also troubled by reports of corruption, by the regime's heavy borrowing to finance its public works projects, and by the slowing of economic growth since these self-appointed saviors of Greece came into power. The Greek economy grew at an average close to 8 per cent a year in the 1960–1966 period, and after the coup at about half that rate. Nevertheless, sufficient prosperity remained at the beginning of the new decade to keep people more interested in their work, recreation, and family life than in stirring up a revolt against their pain-in-the-neck government.

Foreign visitors in this period were impressed by the profound apathy among those whose lives seemed to be not directly touched by the military dictatorship. Some 300,000 demonstrators in Athens did manifest their hostility toward the regime on the occasion of the funeral for George Papandreou, the last elected Prime Minister, in the fall of 1968, but this was an exception to the rule. Most of the people were weary of war, revolutions, and other upheavals. They simply wanted to be left alone to pursue their own objectives without interruption, and the colonels skillfully played upon this feeling to keep themselves in power. Even many of those Greeks who were worried about leaving the dictatorship alone too long, with the danger that it would become further entrenched and that attitudes would tend to polarize with the Communists on one side and the junta on the other, nevertheless seemed to come back to the conclusion that things were not bad enough to justify bloodshed.

The Greek émigrés who were free to air their fears without

danger of reprisals tried to rally their countrymen without significant consequences. Former Prime Minister Caramanlis issued a call in September, 1969, for the army to rebel against the junta, but as *Newsweek* pointed out, "the 'political bombshell' turned out to be more like a pebble thrown into a pond, and by the time the ripples reached Greece, they could hardly be felt." [5] The war of words waged from outside Greece proved to be even less effective than the inept attempt of King Constantine to dislodge the colonels in December, 1967, before he fled to exile in Rome.

One other reason for the apathy seemed to be the new constitution submitted for approval at the polls in September, 1968. Some Greek observers think the new constitution, despite the self-serving provisions written in by the junta, is an improvement over the old one, which had some notable defects. In the junta's plebiscite the constitution won approval from 92.2 per cent of the voters, who were presumably hopeful that it would hasten the restoration of civil liberties. Their hopes were dashed by the continuation of martial law, but the constitution remained in the background as a beacon that might yet light the future.

So long as this situation prevailed the frantic cries for intervention from Washington carried little weight. It is easy to understand why some Greeks would like to shift the blame for conditions in their unhappy land. In this country part of the clamor for a tough American policy that would upset the colonels could be traced to those who eagerly seize any stick to beat the Nixon administration. Practical diplomats, however, were fully aware of the danger that any overt intervention on the part of Washington might rally support behind the colonels. And if they should be toppled, the United States would get the full blame for the subsequent chaos until a democratic government could be established. There is a big question as to whether it is ever possible to restore

[5] *Newsweek*, January 19, 1970, p. 37.

democratic institutions by outside manipulations, for any regime acquiring power by this means is certain to be regarded as the tool of foreign interests seeking to impose their will on the country. A venture to install in Greece the kind of government Washington thinks it should have could prove as disastrous as the Bay of Pigs.

Yet the NATO powers as a whole have an unmistakable interest in saving their eastern flank from disintegration. The Greek imbroglio is a tragedy for Europe and the entire free world. It has tended not only to weaken the actual physical defenses of the west but also to undermine its morale and bring into question the validity of the concept of freedom-loving peoples in different lands standing together for their security. In this sense what happened in Greece is not alone a national phenomenon but an event of profound international concern. Its international implications cannot be ignored without grave damage to NATO and all that it stands for. Somehow the powers that devised this new venture in collective security will have to find a way of lending collective political strength — no less than military defense — to their associates.

The best move made in 1969 to hasten the return of Greece to the democratic fold was the ouster of the Athens government from the Council of Europe. Pressure on the junta began to build up after the council's Commission on Human Rights reported in a confidential document that the colonels "officially tolerated" an "administrative practice" of ill-treatment and torture of political prisoners.[6] As the council assembled in Paris in December, 1969, twelve of its members, including Britain, Denmark, Norway, Sweden, the Netherlands, Belgium, and Italy, were reported ready to vote for the suspension of Greece. Actually, the Greek Foreign Minister, Panayotis Pipinelis, stalked out of the council to give the appearance that his country was initiating the divorce, but his

[6] *Washington Post,* December 10, 1969, p. A28.

anticipation of what was coming did not change the underlying facts. The council had courageously faced the necessity
of denying membership to a government that no longer met
the qualifications of adhering to democratic principles.

The pressure thus applied to bring Greece out of her aberration was clearly distinguishable from any attempted dictation from Washington or any other single western capital.
The Council of Europe was organized in 1949 by the Treaty
of London as an instrument for the promotion of unity
among the democratic nations of Europe. Article 3 of the
council's statute requires all members to "accept the principles of the rule of law and of the enjoyment by all persons
within its jurisdiction of human rights and fundamental
freedoms." The ineligibility of Greece, under this article, had
been clearly demonstrated. In pressing the case against
Greece, the West German Foreign Minister, Walter Scheel,
told the council that "the credibility of this organization is
at stake," [7] and nothing that the Greek spokesman had to say
could change that fact. The colonels at Athens could doubtless have avoided the humiliation at Paris by fixing a date
for new elections and a return to constitutional government
in Greece. Their failure to do so left them further exposed
to every wind of discontent that blows.

The American effort to restrain the Council of Europe
in this salutary stand is difficult to defend. Apparently there
was some fear that if the council soundly spanked the colonels
they might pull out of NATO as well as the council, but this
fear proved to be groundless, and if the junta had chosen
to go it alone, defensewise, that decision might well have
hastened the day when Greece could return to full association with her allies, with a government worthy of her traditions and in line with the aspirations of her people.

After the arrival of Ambassador Tasca in Athens the
United States sought, not to overturn the junta or dictate a

[7] *New York Times,* December 13, 1969, p. 1.

successor, but to persuade the colonels to let democracy emerge once more. If all the NATO powers are consistent in applying such diplomatic pressure, they may be successful in the end. But NATO as an organization also has a vital interest in the preservation of freedom along with collective security. It could properly have followed up the discipline initiated by the Council of Europe. Many thoughtful observers believe that it must do so if it is to survive as a political entity with principles and conscience enough to command the loyalty of free peoples.

Something might be lost if NATO pressured the colonels for the restoration of human rights and elective government to the point of causing the Athens regime to withdraw. The big radio transmitters on Rhodes would be missed. NATO planes now using Greek bases would doubtless have to be shifted to Italy and Turkey or replaced by carriers in the Mediterranean. Suda Bay in Crete would no longer be available to the 6th Fleet. Much greater losses, however, would be suffered by Greece herself. It is impossible to believe that the Greek people would long pay the price of isolation from their natural allies and exposure to the machinations of Communism for the sake of maintaining a handful of naive and unscrupulous usurpers in power.

In the long run NATO will have to improve the insulation it affords to its members against risks of this kind. The disintegration and confusion that led to the colonels' takeover should have engaged the attention of NATO long before the coup became a fait accompli. Surely an organization that can assemble military forces from fifteen nations for their mutual protection could devise means of helping weak governments improve their stability without impairing the rights of their people. Here is a great challenge to those who are seeking to develop greater cohesiveness and new political instrumentalities within the alliance.

It is not to be supposed that any free and independent country will tolerate international dictation as to its domestic affairs. But peoples who seek the protection of an alliance such as NATO must be made to understand that the collective shield will not cover tyranny, torture, and repression. There is a vast difference between trying to force all free governments into the same mold and allowing dictatorship to claim the benefits of collective security intended for only democratic lands. If small countries in the free world are going to claim the enormous advantage of a common defense against subversion and aggression, they will have to forgo the luxury, if such it is, of petty revolutions and repressive minority rule.

Probably this will entail closer cultural and economic ties and evolution toward greater similarities in the political institutions of the allied countries. At least there must be acceptance of common ideals and objectives. If NATO is to hold together as an instrument for the maintenance of peace that will be tolerable to free peoples, it cannot indulge the incongruities that are often accepted in a wartime alliance that may reflect a desperate bid for survival. The very fact that NATO is now looking toward new responsibilities as a peacemaker as well as a guardian of free peoples makes it imperative for it to uphold standards among its own members. It must not be allowed to become a mockery of the principles it seeks to defend. In the short run it can afford to be cautious and understanding of disruptive domestic conditions; it can exhaust persuasion before laying down ultimatums to its members. Yet it cannot escape the obligation of keeping its members in line with the elementary principles of representative government and human rights without risking disintegration of the foundation on which collective security rests in the western world.

XII

Strange New Alliance
in the Far East

RELATIONS BETWEEN the United States and Japan are at once a source of hope and of profound questioning. In the three decades since Pearl Harbor, Japan has become one of our closest friends and allies. Since history reeks with irony, we should not be surprised that this is so, but we need to be aware of the fact that the evolution that produced this result is still running at full tilt. It could greatly enhance the security of American interests in the Far East and the outlook for peace in that part of the world, or it could take a new ironic turn in the opposite direction.

For Japan, the postwar era has been broken into four rather distinct periods. The United States' occupation of that country after the so-called unconditional surrender of 1945 lasted until the negotiation of a peace treaty and a security treaty in 1952. During the next eight years the Treaty of Mutual Cooperation and Security was in force, marking another stage in Japan's resumption of control over her future. A third period marked by increasing Japanese restlessness ended in November, 1969, when President Nixon and Prime Minister Eisaku Sato agreed to return administrative rights over Okinawa to Japan by 1972. This seemed to inaugurate a period of good relations. The importance that Japan attached to the agreement was indicated by the comment of Foreign Minister Kiichi Aichi that ". . . our strength will have been made whole again, and we will be ready for our responsibilities." [1]

Japan's political rehabilitation has been accompanied by an almost miraculous economic recovery. After five years of rapid growth in the latter half of the 1960s, Japan appeared to be heading toward a gross national product of $300 billion by 1975. As the new decade began she was already third among the industrial nations of the world, outranked by only the United States and the Soviet Union and substantially ahead of West Germany and Britain. Some observers of what is happening in Japan conclude that she will head the world in the twenty-first century. James C. Abegglen points to Japan's investment of some 34 per cent of her gross national product in new capital, to produce a current growth rate of 10 to 14 per cent, with roughly a 33 per cent return on investment, as an economic breakthrough of the first order. "Japan's economic system," he writes, "would appear to be the most efficient in the world for generating high productivity." [2]

Up to this point, therefore, the partnership that evolved out of the holocaust of the forties appears to be a remarkable success. Japan has regirded herself for a major role in the Far East, and she is closely tied to the United States in a security arrangement that could have a long-range stabilizing influence on that part of the world. But the realists are still very cautious in their appraisals. They recognize that the euphoria evolving out of the American–Japanese partnership may be at its apex. The certainties about this strange alliance are that it will not remain static and that its future trends cannot now be foreshadowed with any degree of assurance.

Much will depend upon what happens in Okinawa. In the

[1] *Foreign Affairs,* October, 1969, p. 37.
[2] James C. Abegglen in the *Washington Post,* March 15, 1970, p. B3.

period preceding the Nixon-Sato agreement sentiment against
the American presence in Japan and Okinawa was mounting
rapidly. Demonstrations against the operation of B–52 bombers from Okinawa became commonplace. Just before Sato's
1969 visit to the United States 20,000 persons joined in a
parade that ended at one of the American installations on
Okinawa. U. Alexis Johnson, Under Secretary of State for
Political Affairs, confessed to the Symington subcommittee
investigating American commitments abroad that something
had to give:

> I do not think that we could have maintained ourselves
> over the next 5 to 10 years, let us say, in either Japan or
> Okinawa unless we had settled this question of the administra-
> tion of Okinawa. I think the agitation in Okinawa itself as
> well as the agitation in Japan itself would have been greater.
> We would have been out of both places sooner than we other-
> wise would.[3]

There were many irritants besides the presence of B–52s.
One of the foremost problems in Japan proper stemmed from
the fact that the burgeoning urbanization in the vicinity of
Tokyo surrounded some of the military bases. About 70 per
cent of the 75,000 acres occupied by American military installations in 1969 were located within sixty miles of Tokyo,
now the largest city in the world. In this same area 77 per
cent of the American military personnel in Japan and their
families were stationed, meaning something more than 71,000
persons. The Air Force base at Yokota, for example, became
the target of numerous protests because of the noise it created
after a Tokyo suburb grew up around it. After studying a
map showing the cluster of American military bases on the

[3] "United States Security Agreements and Commitments Abroad: Japan and
Okinawa," hearings before the Subcommittee on United States Security Agreements and Commitments Abroad of the Senate Committee on Foreign Relations, 91st Cong., 2nd sess. (Washington: Government Printing Office, 1970),
p. 1243.

Kanto Plain, which is Tokyo's metropolitan area, Roland A. Paul of the Symington subcommittee commented:

What this means in American terms would be that there would be three foreign military bases, one major foreign naval base, a dozen or more minor facilities, four golf courses reserved for the use or the pleasure of foreign military personnel, and an exclusive downtown hotel, all in something similar to the New York metropolitan area. I equate it with New York, not just because of the similarity in population size but also because, as New York could be said to be the hub of our commercial activity, the United States being the greatest economic power in the world, Tokyo is even more so the hub of the second greatest commercial power in the free world, with all that means for congestion of commercial aircraft and ground transportation.[4]

One of the most notable irritants was the Mito Bombing Range, which was used for pilot and air-crew training. Pilots stationed at Yokota Air Base in the Tokyo suburbs used the Mito Bombing Range to practice their dive bombing, air-ground gunnery, skip bombing, and so forth because the range was close to Yokota. The troublesome factor was that the bombing range was also only 2.6 miles from a plutonium research and development laboratory operated by the Japan Atomic Fuel Corporation and within three miles of two Japanese resorts, Owarai and Ajigaura Beaches. Precautions were taken to avoid accidents, but some "bomblets" were inadvertently released outside of the Mito Range. On February 27, 1968, when a pilot placed the armament switches to arm his gun, the trigger safety mechanism malfunctioned and the gun began to fire indiscriminately on this narrowly pinched range. The Japanese cabinet voted to relocate the range, and it was finally closed in 1970.

Sharp questions have also been raised about the continued

[4] Ibid., p. 1232.

use of Itazuki Air Base where 880 United States personnel were stationed in 1970. Military officials defended the spending of $4,672,000 in three years at Itazuki by saying that it was an important "forward operating location and contingency base during periods of international crisis," but the record showed that only 37 per cent of the traffic over a three-year period had been U.S. military planes. The other 63 per cent was Japanese civil traffic, for Itazuki is basically a civilian airport for the city of Fukuoka. Yet the entire expense of operating this facility fell upon the United States until an agreement for reduced U.S. flying operations and for cost-sharing at Itazuki went into effect in June, 1971.

On June 2, 1968, an RF-4C flying out of Itazuki lost control on a landing approach and crashed into the fifth floor of a building under construction on the campus of Kyushu University. Both pilots ejected safely and no Japanese nationals were injured. Nevertheless, a furor was raised. Students attacked a U.S. Air Force vehicle carrying investigative and security personnel. Housewives, fearing their families were in danger, joined leftist elements in demonstrations. University officials announced that the crashing plane had narrowly missed a building containing radioactive cobalt. Further agitation for removal of the base broke out when an RF-101 crashed nearby and another RF-101 crashed on take-off. In June, 1969, the United States ambassador announced that no jet aircraft would thereafter operate from Itazuki, but the agitation continued for several months until the symbol of the struggle — the remains of the ruined plane on Kyushu University campus — was removed more than sixteen months after the crash had occurred.

In the Symington subcommittee hearing, counsel asked Lieutenant General Thomas K. McGehee why 880 personnel were needed to support a civilian airport for the purpose of a contingency base for operations into Korea. The base was going to be there as a civilian airport, in any event, he said.[5] The answer was that if the United States relinquished the base it would have no reentry rights. So an expensive operation was kept going, despite its irritation to the Japanese, because of the remote possibility that it might be useful in some future crisis in Korea. Apparently no effort had been made to induce the Japanese to share the expenses of operation. The incident became a very pointed symbol of the overextension of our military facilities abroad, with little regard for the cost or the consequences.

Another item of interest to the Symington subcommittee was the Tama Ammunition Depot, a 492-acre "facility" that had formerly been a royal hunting preserve. The Japanese had converted it into a naval ordnance depot in 1922. In 1970 the American military was using it as a golf course, a Boy Scout summer camp, and a religious retreat. Because of the great pressure in Japan for living space, there was talk of a housing development on Tama and some negotiations had taken place, but the military was not in a hurry to act. In the Symington subcommittee hearing this exchange is recorded:

> MR. PAUL . . . A few minutes ago, General, you talked in terms of the Japanese envisaging down the road a planned community out there [at Tama]. Why can't they have it? Why shouldn't it be part of the negotiation?
> GENERAL McGEHEE. I think it will be.
> MR. PAUL. To turn it back?
> GENERAL McGEHEE. In due time. There is no pressure at the present time.[6]

The Symington subcommittee staff, which had made a careful study of the problem, felt that the U.S. military

[5] Ibid., p. 1271.
[6] Ibid., p. 1266.

should be pulling out of the Kanto Plain, which is already a megalopolis. Through its counsel, Roland A. Paul, the subcommittee suggested that Yokota Air Base be released to Japan for commercial traffic and that its military functions be transferred to Misawa, where more space is available. Yokota is estimated to be worth more than $40 million to the Japanese. The Pentagon did shift all the F-4s based at Yokota to Okinawa in 1971 and returned a reconnaissance unit to the United States, but other extensive operations at Yokota continued. The F-4s on Misawa were relocated in Korea, but the Air Force also continued flying there on a reduced scale.

The larger question is whether the United States should retain military bases indefinitely at any point in Japan proper. Several exchanges at the Symington subcommittee hearings threw some light on the problem:

SENATOR [CLIFFORD] CASE. . . . Look, we are not going to stay in Japan, are we? How long is it going to take these people to get on their own feet and take on their own burdens? This is a hearing in which we are not talking to the world at large. We are talking to each other and we both have responsibilities here. The Armed Services have, the State Department has, and the Congress has, and I think the people of the country are generally entitled to know how long this thing is going to last.
MR. JOHNSON [Under Secretary of State and former Ambassador to Japan]. I really could not put, you know, an exact time frame on it. As we were previously discussing, our position in Japan is related to our position in Korea. How long are we going to maintain American forces in Korea, how long do we intend to maintain the 7th Fleet out in that part of the world in relationship to our obligations out there, including Taiwan and the rest of the area —
SENATOR SYMINGTON. If the Secretary will yield, we are not talking about the 7th Fleet.

MR. JOHNSON. I say the presence of the 7th Fleet though is related to our presence in Japan.

SENATOR SYMINGTON. The oceans are an entirely different breed of cat than the occupation of foreign countries. Oceans are available to all people who want to put their money in ships.

MR. JOHNSON. But I was relating our fleet presence out there to our presence in the Yokosuka base, the Yokosuka and Sasebo bases, as part of the support of our fleet there.

SENATOR SYMINGTON. I want the record to be clear. We do not necessarily need those bases to maintain a fleet in the Far East.

MR. JOHNSON. No, we could — there are lot of things we could do . . .[7]

At another point in the hearing Secretary Johnson's assertion that "you need the back-up of your Japanese and Okinawa bases" if the commitment in Korea is to be maintained brought this response:

SENATOR SYMINGTON. We were told when we went into Korea we would be there for a short time; but we have been there for . . . 20 years, next June 26 . . . I do not think we have to have so many islands in the Pacific to back up Korea. The Philippines back them up, Okinawa backs them up, Taiwan backs them up, Japan backs them up, the Polaris submarines back them up.

How many places do you have to back them up before you break your own back? This is [my] thinking as I watch the value of the dollar steadily disintegrate at the same time interest rates go up . . .

MR. JOHNSON. Well, if we are going to keep the 7th Fleet out in that part of the world —

SENATOR FULBRIGHT. One thing leads to another.[8]

The argument seemed to boil down to the fact that the maintenance of costly, friction-producing bases in Japan,

[7] Ibid., p. 1261.
[8] Ibid., p. 1235.

after that country has assumed full responsibility for its own conventional defense, is a matter of convenience to the American military. Will the pursuit of that convenience poison the future relations between the two countries? Up to now the willingness of the United States to yield a point when tension in Japan has mounted has been enough to maintain fairly good relations between the two countries, but this may not always be so.

There is some comfort for both the Japanese and apprehensive Americans in the progressive liquidation of the bases established in the postwar years. In 1957 the Air Force returned its Chitose base in Hokkaido to Japan and has since reduced its major operating bases from seven to one — Yokota. In addition the Air Force has a major support base at Tachikawa, and Itazuki on Kyushu is used for logistics. The Navy has shifted most of its activities to the Naval Operating Base at Sasebo, but it also retains substantial facilities in the Yokosuka-Yokohama Complex. The Marines operate a naval station at Iwakuni in the southern part of Japan, near Hiroshima. The Army has a headquarters base, Camp Zuma, and Sagami Depot. All the other American bases in operation in 1970 were relatively small installations. Since 1952 the Americans have reduced the land area they hold from 270,000 to less than 75,000 acres and the number of "facilities" from 3800 to 125. American military personnel in the Islands has been trimmed from about 260,000 at the height of the Korean war (1951) to 41,000 in early 1970 and to possibly 25,000 in 1971.

Nevertheless, the American presence in Japan is still substantial, and the rate of curtailment is often exaggerated. Spokesmen for the State Department made a good deal of the cutback resulting from a study initiated in 1968. Out of a "54 facilities package," they said, 23 facilities were returned to the Japanese. When the Symington subcommittee looked into this supposedly remarkable feat of withdrawal, however, it found that the returned facilities occupied only 2.5 per cent of the total areas held by the Americans. Despite the cutbacks, the Pentagon estimated in 1970 that the annual outlay for the American military in Japan, including salaries, amounted to $490 million.

Incidentally, the Misawa Air Base in northern Japan, which is closely associated with two forward-operating locations in Korea, is only 250 miles from the Kuril Island chain held by the Soviet Union and 450 miles from the Vladivostok area. A comparable Soviet base in Communist Cuba would be regarded as an intolerable threat to the security of the United States.

Aside from the bases we still hold on Japan proper, the bastion on Okinawa is formidable. Okinawa is strategically located about midway between Tokyo to the north and Manila to the south. It is only 400 miles from Taiwan, yet far enough from the coast of China to be relatively secure from attack. Seoul is about 750 miles away to the north and Saigon about 1750 miles to the south. On this almost impregnable island in the Ryukyu chain the United States has built an early-warning radar system, the hub of an extensive communications network, and a logistical base that can provide sustained support to deploy a force of 500,000 men. The U.S. government holds about 75,000 acres of land on the island, mostly under lease, on which it has invested about three-quarters of a billion dollars.

Lieutenant General James B. Lampert, High Commissioner of the Ryukyu Islands and Commanding General of the U.S. Army there, has described Okinawa as "the best location for stationing a quick reaction force for use in the Western Pacific." [9] Troops stationed there were the first American support and combat units sent to Vietnam. B-52s

[9] Ibid., p. 1292.

and other aircraft are refueled by tankers operating from
Kadena Air Base, one of the largest Air Force installations
in the world. Kadena handles a wide variety of aircraft on
a continuous basis. Its operations are supplemented by Naha
Air Force Base, a center for defense and transport aircraft
and a base for naval aviation. Naha Port has ten deep-water
berths and a beach that will accommodate five LSTs. The
Navy on Okinawa also supplies provisions and fuel to ships
of the 7th Fleet. A major relay station operated by the Voice
of America on Okinawa keeps North China, the Soviet Far
East, Korea, and Japan aware of what is transpiring in the
United States.

The promise to return administrative rights in Okinawa
to Japan has not revolutionized the relationship between
Washington and Tokyo, but it has notably altered the evolving partnership. The Okinawa bases will continue to be
used by the United States, but air operations have been
reduced at Naha and Onna Point, with the anticipated release of 5000 men, military and civilian. Under the new
arrangement, Japan will have a voice in how the Okinawa
bases are to be used. The terms of the 1960 mutual security
treaty, which President Nixon and Premier Sato agreed to
maintain indefinitely as part of their 1970 understanding,
will become applicable to Okinawa as well as to Japan
proper. Nuclear weapons are thus banned from Okinawa.
All "nukes" on the island when the agreement was reached
had to be removed, and the future deployment of such
weapons there was forbidden unless the Japanese government should give its consent.

Viewed in only these terms the agreement seemed to involve major United States concessions for very little in
return. Potentially far more important, however, was Japan's
acceptance of a new role in the defense of free Asia. In the
past the Japanese had seemed merely to tolerate the American presence in their country as a consequence of their de-

feat in World War II and in return for current security behind the American nuclear shield. In the new understanding that became a part of the Okinawa package Japan assumed a limited role in the preservation of peace in the Pacific. Tokyo is no longer insisting on complete detachment from international security problems. The great industrial complex that is Japan is back in the ring — not as a military power but as a useful influence of great potential in the promotion of stability in the western Pacific.

Prime Minister Sato spelled out the significance of this phase of the agreement in his speech at the National Press Club in Washington on November 21, 1969. "The biggest problem in the negotiations between Japan and the United States for the return of the islands," he said, "was nothing more nor less than the role that Okinawa was playing in the maintenance of peace. Japan and the United States agree in their basic recognition of the importance of United States military bases on Okinawa. The peace-keeping function of the bases on Okinawa must continue to be kept effective."

Sato welcomed renewal of the United States–Japan Security Treaty primarily as a means of ensuring the security of his own country. But he also recognized that "in the real international world it is impossible to adequately maintain the security of Japan without international peace and security of the Far East. This is where the second objective of the Japan–United States Security Treaty comes to the foreground — the cooperation of Japan and the United States in the form of the use of facilities and areas in Japan by United States forces under Article VI thereof for the security of the Far East in a broader context. And it would be in accord with our national interest for us to determine our response to prior consultation regarding the use of these facilities and areas in the light of the need to maintain the security of the Far East, including Japan."

Japan's security would be "seriously affected," Sato

acknowledged, by an armed attack against the Republic of Korea or the Taiwan area. The Japanese Prime Minister seemed to be saying that, in all probability, Japan would permit the use of nuclear weapons from its territory if necessary for defense of the Far East. He pictured Japan as having broken out of a "closed" relationship with the United States, confined to the solution of bilateral problems, and having entered into an "open" relationship in which the two countries would work together for broad international objectives. Japan's special role, as Sato outlined it, is not in the military sphere, except for defense of the homeland, but "in such fields as economic and technical assistance towards the nation-building efforts of the Asian countries." In the afterglow of enthusiasm that followed the Okinawa agreement he held out hope that "the two great nations across the Pacific, of quite different ethnic and historical backgrounds, are on the verge of starting a great historical experiment in working together for a new order in the world, on a dimension that transcends a bilateral alliance." [10]

This may seem to be an excessively euphoric view of an undertaking launched by two countries that were mortal enemies only a quarter century ago. It is not, however, more optimistic than some other comments from objective sources. The agreement for the return of Okinawa to Japan was widely hailed as an act of extraordinary statesmanship. The *Washington Post* called it "a mutual boon of the first order." [11] Every observer of events in the Far East knew that President Nixon had to decide as he did if the United States was to retain the friendship and good will of the Japanese people. Without the return of Okinawa, there would have been no future for Japanese-American partnership. Never-

[10] Prime Minister Eisaku Sato's address to the National Press Club, November 21, 1969.
[11] Issue of November 23, 1969, p. B6.

theless, the United States did pay the price for cooperation instead of trying to get by with repression or imperialism. The policy freely adopted by the two governments stands out in striking contrast to that pursued by the Soviet Union, which continues to hold the Japanese territories it took in World War II.

When the great potential of this course has been fully recognized, however, the hurdles still ahead must be kept in perspective. In many respects the alliance is strained and fragile. The third most powerful nation in the world, industrially speaking, is partly dependent for its security on bases maintained on its soil by a former enemy. How long will the emerging Japan, with its fantastic 10 to 14 per cent growth rate, be willing to play a subordinate role in the international scene? Some Japanese leaders are now openly advocating that their country become a nuclear power, and it unquestionably has the capacity to do so. The government itself is steadily expanding its military program despite the U.S.-imposed Article 9 of the Japanese postwar constitution that renounces war "forever" and pledges that "land, sea and air forces, as well as other war potential, will never be maintained." Prime Minister Sato interpreted his landslide victory at the polls early in 1970 as a mandate for increased military spending "in accordance with our national power and circumstances." [12]

At the time of the Nixon-Sato agreement Japan had 240,000 men in its Self-Defense Forces, including 180,000 ground troops, a navy consisting of 210 ships of approximately 125,000 tons, and an air force of 960 planes. If the five-year plan originally conceived for the years 1972–1976 should be carried out, these forces would be doubled. Sato's minister of state for defense once urged the allocation of at least 2 per cent of GNP to the military, which would mean a

[12] Selig S. Harrison in the *Washington Post*, February 15, 1970, p. 1.

step up from $1.25 billion to $4.4 billion in 1972 and $6.8 billion by 1976. Later he toned down this recommendation, but some Japanese hawks call for a much steeper climb of military spending to reach about 6 per cent of GNP by the middle of the decade.

With larger security forces in being, is it reasonable to suppose that Japan will long continue to eschew a world-power role? Some crystal-ball gazers think Japan's subordinate role may last another ten years. It is worthy of note, however, that Yasuhiro Nakasone, who was chosen minister of state for the Defense Agency after the great sweep of the Liberal Democratic Party in the wake of the Okinawa agreement, favors "a basic reexamination of the Japan–U.S. defense relationship" by 1975. The people appear to be strongly opposed to any involvement of their country in war or a posture that might lead to war. Militarism is still associated in the public mind with fascism and repression. Nevertheless, shifts in Japan's postwar pacifism are evident on a wide scale. The big question that no one seems able to answer yet is whether Japan can find a satisfying role commensurate with her advanced economic status but short of the development of air, naval, and nuclear weapons that would rival the superpowers. The strong hope of the peace forces in Asia and elsewhere is that she can and that her contribution to the development of the Far East will lie chiefly in economic and technological aid and the expansion of commerce.

If this hope is to be realized, a lasting association with the United States seems to be imperative. Only the U.S.A. can provide the nuclear insurance and the naval shield essential to allow some degree of freedom among the emerging nations of Asia in working out their destiny. But the partnership between Washington and Tokyo for this purpose would have to be something more than mere American use of Japanese facilities for the perpetuation of U.S. military dominance in the Far East. It would have to evolve into a genuine cooperative system in which the allies would participate in the decision-making process no less than in supplying arms, men, and facilities.

There may be more ifs on the eastern side of the Pacific than on the western. Many Americans are concerned by the spectacle of Japan, with only minuscule defense expenditures, growing rich while taxpayers on this side of the Pacific shoulder staggering taxes or inflationary deficits to cover the cost of defending freedom in Asia. Up to 1970 while Japan was keeping its spending on arms well below 1 per cent of its gross national product, the United States was spending about 8.3 per cent of its GNP for the military. But Japan has shown some interest in participating in an international peace-keeping force, especially if the United Nations should set up such a force for Southeast Asia. Without risking any return to militarism, Japan could also contribute immeasurably to stability and peace in the Far East with a massive economic aid program and liberal trade regulations that would help to even the input into a Western Pacific partnership.

One other factor that will help to restrain any resurgence of militarism or imperialism in Japan is the attitude of her Asian neighbors. Korea, the Philippines, Burma, Malaysia, and other countries with vivid memories of World War II are loath to have Japan assume any responsibility for their security. The agreement to return Okinawa to Japan brought expressions of concern from some Nationalist Chinese officials who noted that it "would move the Japanese border some hundreds of miles closer to Taiwan." [13] But most of the Far East outside of Communist China would doubtless welcome a collective security arrangement into

[13] Philip Shabecoff in the *New York Times*, December 18, 1969.

which Japan could be integrated somewhat as Western Germany has been integrated into NATO.

However the details may be worked out, Japan's presence as a virile industrial power in a regional defense system could be a powerful incentive to peace. If her own strength should continue to be predominantly centered in the economic sphere, she would doubtless be reluctant to resort to force. Her leanings would logically be toward negotiations, conciliation, and a live-and-let-live attitude that might well restrain the impetuosity that has often marked American policy in these matters in the past. The prevailing attitude of the Japanese toward the war in Vietnam, for example, has been one of hoping for success of Saigon's efforts to maintain its independent status, with American help, but yet of concern that the war might spread to Japan. If Japan had been at a conference table to consider the course to be taken in Vietnam back in the middle sixties, it is quite possible that the Lyndon Johnson regime in Washington might have been saved from its worst blunders of escalation.

The risks along the road the two countries have chosen to travel must be faced with candor and foresight. The Japanese people, about 100 million strong, are a proud and nationalistic race. One eminent leader has said that, as a self-respecting nation, Japan must become responsible for its own defense, but he worries about the outcome because he "cannot be sure where we will stop." [14] Foreseeing enormous growth in the years ahead, Herman Kahn, director of the Hudson Institute, has predicted that Japan will "look for prestige" and is therefore likely to become the world's sixth nuclear power.[15] He expects Japan to insist on a status equal to or just below the places occupied by the United States and the Soviet Union and to seek and obtain a permanent seat

[14] Takashi Oka in the *New York Times,* February 20, 1970, p. C14.
[15] Emerson Chapin in the *New York Times,* December 7, 1969, p. 8L

on the United Nations Security Council. James C. Abegglen, Vice President of the Boston Consulting Group, which operates in Tokyo, extrapolates from Japan's phenomenal growth rate, five times that of the United States, that "within a generation, it [Japan] may well be the world's most affluent society." [16]

In any event it will not be a problem of holding Japan to a role preconceived for her in Washington. Japan herself will make the choice. The question on this side of the Pacific is whether America will be sufficiently flexible and cooperative to retain the trust and good will of Japan in her rejuvenated status. The best advice that has been given to date seems to come from former ambassador Edwin O. Reischauer, who holds that "our relationship with Japan is absolutely crucial. Japan is more important to us than all the rest of Asia." [17] Complementary to that conclusion is the ambassador's view that the United States' military role in Asia can be only marginal — to preserve freedom of the seas, to promote an external environment of stability, and, functioning as a reserve force, to discourage blatant aggression.

More than a year before his election, President Nixon was also concerned about holding the friendship of Japan. Writing in *Foreign Affairs,* he said:

> Not to trust Japan today with its own armed forces and with responsibility for its own defense would be to place its people and its government under a disability which, whatever its roots in painful recent history, ill accords with the role Japan must play in helping secure the common safety of noncommunist Asia.[18]

[16] Ibid.; see also Abegglen's article in the *Washington Post,* March 15, 1970, p. B1.
[17] Quoted in the *Christian Science Monitor,* June 24, 1969.
[18] Richard M. Nixon in *Foreign Affairs,* October, 1967, pp. 120–121.

In his so-called state-of-the-world message to Congress he acknowledged that the return of Okinawa "was among the most important decisions I have taken as President" and that "our cooperation with Japan will be crucial to our efforts to help other Asian nations develop in peace." [19]

The alternative to close and friendly ties with an emergent Japan would be either the abandonment of American interests in the Western Pacific or an attempt to go it alone. Either course might prove disastrous. A great power cannot suddenly withdraw into a protective shell without leaving chaos in the wake of its retreat and inviting its own dissolution. Japan and perhaps India would be virtually forced to acquire nuclear arms, thus dooming the nuclear nonproliferation treaty. The resulting turmoil and danger of a world holocaust would almost certainly recoil upon ourselves, with further disruption of our social and political equilibrium. In this age of superpowers, super weapons, and multipolarization the safest course for a great democratic country appears to lie in sharing power with other free peoples and trusting collective arrangements, even though they may not always produce the results that an impetuous President may have in mind.

The fact that no one can foresee all the consequences of such a venture is no argument against it. The great uncertainties of life justify neither infanticide nor adult suicide. The future of the Washington-Tokyo alignment will have to evolve out of the common interests the two countries share. If the American concession to the common interest involves the abandonment of all our military bases in Japan, it will be a small price to pay for keeping the alliance in good repair. What is obvious at this point is that steering these mutual efforts into constructive channels in the Pacific is

[19] United States Foreign Policy for the 1970's, Report by President Richard Nixon to the Congress, February 18, 1970.

second in importance only to the maintenance of a virile and alert NATO in the Atlantic community of nations.

Japan's announcement of her decision to extend indefinitely her security treaty with the United States in June, 1970, met with relatively little opposition. Some left-wing students put on a show, but the return of Okinawa had "defanged" the security treaty issue. Many other irritants remained, however, as the riot inside Kadena Air Base in December, 1970, demonstrated. Okinawans had been aroused when a U.S. military court had freed a serviceman charged with killing a pedestrian. When a car driven by another GI struck an Okinawan and left him lying in the street, an infuriated mob invaded the base, burned eighty-two cars, damaged a school, and inflicted a heavy toll of injuries. These incidents were followed in January, 1971, by a crisis over the removal of 13,000 tons of poison gas from the island. Major differences also arose over the desire of the Okinawans and their Japanese leaders to recover a large part of the 72,900 acres of land on the island occupied by the American military bases. Other forces in both countries assailed the alliance in the name of peace and the protection of home industry.

Statesmen of high courage and wisdom in both Washington and Tokyo will have to keep their eyes on the central objectives if this hopeful experiment is to live up to its favorable beginning.

XIII

Trying to Look Ahead

WHERE SHOULD WE be tending in this age of nuclear weapons, superpowers, and ideological hostility? Can we hope for security without trying to put down every left-wing uprising that breaks out any place in the world? Is there a safer or more promising alternative to our military posture astride the globe? Can we find a rational middle ground between withdrawal into what is generally called Fortress America and attempting to dominate every international sphere? Will the shock of retreat and possible failure in Vietnam impair our self-confidence or stimulate belligerence in some other direction by way of smothering humiliation?

Obviously, much fresh thinking about our relation to the world around us is in order — not the wild gyrations of the revolutionists but the sober reflections of statesmen who are well grounded in the traditional American ideals and also alert to the realities of the 1970s. We need to recognize the mistakes of the past without being intimidated or misguided by them. The discovery that the world is not our oyster, to be wheedled or subdued, could lead to grave demoralization or to a wise regeneration of strength, depending upon what the national reaction to it is.

The foundation for a new policy must be, in my opinion,

a less formidable military posture in the world. The role of world policeman has led us into intolerable complications and tarnished the image that we Americans had acquired in the years following World War II as a benevolent and peace-loving people. In the interval we have talked peace and practiced war. For a few years the name of the United States was synonymous with the magnificent Marshall Plan, but more recently our friends as well as our enemies abroad identify American policy with the war in Korea, the occupation of the Dominican Republic, the Bay of Pigs, the war in Vietnam, the secret war in Laos, and the invasion of the Cambodian sanctuaries. The facts that these military operations were undertaken for worthy purposes and that some of them may have contributed to freedom and stability in countries accustomed to neither tend to be obscured by the pervasive nature of our military responses. For better or for worse, we have acquired the image of a superpower consistently trying to achieve its goals by resort to military force.

Probably the most pessimistic view is that this excessive reliance on military power is inherent in our nature — that red-blooded he-men in a powerful free land are simply indulging their craving for the excitement and the rituals of war. Professors Robin Fox and Lionel Tiger of Rutgers University have developed the thesis that warring is "an example of a behavioral heritage which once served us well but which we now serve." Man is still the hunter, responding to primitive instincts. "Industrial man," they say, "is barely out of the evolutionary womb — a 200-year-old babe trying to squander a two-million-year-old inheritance." Irrational though it may be in these days of nuclear weapons, they argue that

> War taps certain basic emotions such as loyalty, self-sacrifice, comradeship, aggression, pleasure in activity and delight in

killing skills which were part of the evolving behavioral repertoire of our hunting-fighting ancestors.[1]

In line with this thesis one might speculate that our wars of the twentieth century have come to be a substitute for the frontier that dominated our psychology and our way of life in the nineteenth. But the problem does not vanish with recognition that the hunter instinct and the violence of the frontier still color our heritage. The law of life is that species must adapt themselves to changing conditions or perish. The nuclear arsenals of the superpowers are an ever-present reminder that civilization cannot survive without drastic restraints upon military force. In the 1970s war is simply not an acceptable or tolerable means of settling international differences. It follows that the United States, instead of leading the militaristic parade, ought to be exerting a powerful suasion toward the dethronement of military power.

Yet we are in fact a highly militarized nation. More than two years ago General Shoup, former Commandant of the United States Marine Corps, noted that "We have an immense and expensive military establishment, fueled by a gigantic defense industry, and millions of proud, patriotic, and frequently bellicose and militaristic citizens." [2] The general also pointed out that the armed forces exert a powerful influence on public opinion; that 20 per cent of our adult population are veterans; that the military establishments maintain powerful lobbies that; "many ambitious military professionals truly yearn for wars and the opportunities for glory and distinction afforded only in combat"; that the rush of American forces to Vietnam was stimulated in part by interservice rivalry; that the bombing in both North and South Vietnam — described as "one of the most wasteful and expensive hoaxes ever to be put over on the American

[1] *Washington Post,* July 6, 1969, p. B5.
[2] "The New American Militarism," *The Atlantic,* April, 1969, p. 51.

people" — was often regarded as "fine experience" for young pilots. Military thinking has been far too large a factor in the making of our foreign policy. The solemn warning of President Eisenhower against allowing the military-industrial complex to wield excessive power has not been taken very seriously.

No one in his right mind would leave our country defenseless in an age when violence is rampant. Nor is there any possibility of slipping back to the good old days before World War I, when we had only the nucleus of a military establishment, or to the blind isolationism that prevailed between the two big wars. Tragic though it is, security in the nuclear age seems to require a "balance of terror" and sufficient conventional strength to make resort to the ultimate weapons improbable. But this does not mean that the most powerful nation in the world must allow its militarism to run riot. We can maintain an adequate defense and buttress our alliances with other free peoples in areas vital to our security without sitting astride the globe and trying to settle every remote controversy by resort to military force.

The pendulum swung too far — from impotence in international affairs to super-policing on three continents and the seven seas. At the close of World War II the United States was the only major area of stability in the free world. It could not close its eyes to the Soviet Union's energetic and ruthless cultivation of chaos for the sake of spreading Communism. But these crusades were often intermingled with nationalistic movements, and the militaristic responses from Washington were often clumsy. In the case of the Dominican Republic the United States seemed to panic at the sight of a Communist shadow. Our overweening preoccupation with putting down Bolshevism continued, moreover, long after the Communist threat of spreading monolithic tyranny over the world had foundered on internal dissensions. Whatever may have been the excuse or justification for our over-extended military operations in the 1950s and 1960s, the conflict between Moscow and Peking and the evaporation of Nikita Khrushchev's threat to bury us brought a shift in the international climate that should be reflected in our own policies.

In the 1970s, therefore, Americans should be clamoring less for military superiority everywhere and more for peace and accommodation. The Nixon administration recognized the desirability of this objective in its emphasis on negotiations and increased cooperation with our allies. Its first two years often conveyed the impression that Washington was still seeking to exploit its position astride the globe, but the rhetoric calls for a "balanced and positive American role" and the trend is toward military curtailment.

A shift on Capitol Hill should accentuate this rehabilitation of the American image abroad. In January, 1971, Senator Allen J. Ellender of Louisiana succeeded the late Senator Richard B. Russell of Georgia as chairman of the Senate Appropriations Committee and of its Defense Subcommittee. Russell had systematically cleared enormous military spending bills. Ellender, by contrast, has made a practice of visiting our military bases abroad as a sort of one-man team seeking to cut unnecessary outlays. Though not a dove, he favors complete withdrawal of American forces from Indochina. Still vigorous at the age of eighty, he is expected to exert a strong influence for trimming the American military presence abroad.

If there is ever to be a real thaw in the cold war, we shall have to take some risks in this direction. The attempt to inaugurate an era of peace supported by American troops in many lands and 400 military bases on every continent comes close to being a self-contradiction. The risks we take in liquidating that policy and pulling back from the brink of a universal paternalism are minor compared to the hazards of further drift into the morass of miscellaneous military interventions. Nothing in these pages exudes one iota of sympathy with isolationism. Even if such a course were possible, it would bring economic disaster and dash the hopes of mankind for some progress toward international controls and an emerging sense of world law and justice. In an age of increasing regionalism, nuclear power, space satellites, and travel to the moon, we could not retreat to the nineteenth century without pulling the pillars of the temple down upon our own heads. The effect would be to turn all the world against the timorous giant who chose to turn away from his neighbors and go it alone. As between dabbling in world constabularism and a retreat to Fortress America, the latter would be far more dangerous. But both are bankrupt ideas that need to be discarded when we talk about where we are going in the 1970s.

Former Secretary of State Rusk thinks we are already tending back toward isolationism. "We face the danger," he said near the end of 1970, "of removing collective security with nothing to put in its place." [3] But the military globalism of the 1960s cannot properly be characterized as collective security. The United States tried to go it alone in Vietnam and the Dominican Republic. The proper alternative to that nationalism running riot is not isolationism but a real sharing of responsibility in the free world that might be described as genuine collective security or prudent partnership. Belatedly we must acknowledge, as President Kennedy did in 1961, that "the United States is neither omnipotent nor omniscient." JFK went on to conclude, in a speech at the University of Washington, that "we cannot right every wrong or reverse each adversity — and that therefore there cannot

[3] *Newsweek*, December 14, 1970, p. 29.

be an American solution to every world problem."[4] It follows from this sound conclusion that a distinction must be drawn between a global police role and genuine collective security.

Several essential elements in this reorientation of American foreign policy may be summarized as follows:

The first step, of course, is to liquidate the military operations on which we embarked without any element of prudent partnership, primarily the war in Indochina. Difficult though this may be, it is an essential preliminary to the emergence of any viable new international policy. We cannot readily make a new start while we remain bogged down in a venture that most of our friends would not touch with a ten-foot pole. As this is written, the Nixon administration is faithfully adhering to its policy of gradual withdrawal from Vietnam, but the roughest part of the journey is yet to come. The American mettle may be severely tested as the last remnants seek a safe exit under possibly hazardous conditions. Yet the risk must be taken to avoid further pursuit of a bankrupt policy which could not in the long run be sustained.

Ultimately, the aim ought to be to withdraw all American troops from the continent of Asia. This would include Korea and Thailand as well as Vietnam and Laos. If those countries wish to protect themselves from Communism, they ought to do it with their own manpower. The logic of Vietnamization that President Nixon set into motion soon after he arrived at the White House is that the United States will not again send ground troops to fight a war on the continent of Asia. As in the case of Vietnam, however, the change has to come as a transition and not as a rout.

Plans for application of this policy to South Korea brought

[4] Arthur Schlesinger, *A Thousand Days: John F. Kennedy in the White House* (Boston: Houghton Mifflin, 1965), p. 615.

a sharp outcry from that country when they came to light in July, 1970. Secretary of Defense Laird let it be known that a sharp cut in the 60,000 American troops then in Korea could be expected in the summer of 1971. In Seoul, Prime Minister Chung II Kwon responded that if the pullout reduced the American forces by 20,000 men, as rumored, he and all members of his cabinet would resign. But Washington went ahead with its planning and Seoul's begging for the Americans to stay provided a salutary contrast to the moaning in Czechoslovakia over the renewed Soviet occupation of that country.

The United States has a security treaty with South Korea. Obviously there was no intention in Washington of inviting a new invasion from the north by suddenly leaving the South Koreans to face their enemies entirely alone. But after seventeen years of an uneasy truce between the two segments of Korea, a major shrinkage in the American presence could scarcely be regarded as unreasonable. In this period the United States had given South Korea military and economic aid amounting to $7,459,900,000 in addition to keeping one American division on the front line as a "tripwire" and one division farther back in reserve. When South Korea sent about 50,000 men to fight in Vietnam, moreover, the United States supported them to the extent of approximately $5000 per man.

During the same period North Korea obtained extensive aid from the Soviet Union but, so far as is known, no Russian armed forces. The North Koreans have a formidable army of their own, estimated at 350,000 men, although it is matched against some 500,000 South Koreans in uniform. With more than twice the population of North Korea and with a far more developed economy, the Republic of Korea should not in the long run have any serious difficulty in maintaining its independence, with continued American economic and arms aid, unless it should be invaded by Russia or China. Certainly American policy should look toward further troop withdrawals as soon as the South Koreans can take over the added burden and toward further internationalization of any remaining shield as soon as that is possible.

The second step in a pullback from globalism could well be a reduction in the number of American bases in other countries. Fortunately, there are some encouraging signs in this area. In December, 1970, the Nixon administration announced that it had closed sixty-eight foreign bases and reduced forty-four more. In some instances the American forces were literally pushed out of bases on which millions had been spent, but other closings resulted from a deliberate policy of narrowing our commitments abroad on the basis of a study made by the National Security Council. The downward trend was thrown into reverse, however, when the United States agreed to build a base for joint use with the British on the island of Diego Garcia in the Indian Ocean "to fill a gap in the system of world-wide United States naval communications." The concept of a global military system seemed to be in full flower again. The Pentagon also clings to many older bases of highly questionable utility when viewed in terms of lost good will and potential military entanglements as well as monetary costs.

Judgments will vary greatly as to how far the liquidation of military bases abroad should go. It is not the purpose of this volume to provide a blueprint — a task for which the author would have no competence. But it should be obvious to every intelligent layman that the ultimate policy to be followed cannot safely be left to the military. The military convenience in maintaining a great array of bases in many different countries is only one aspect of a highly complex international problem, and the military view may be sharply at variance with our long-range national interests.

Most of our problem in regard to bases stems from the fact that military decisions have often escaped broad-gauged, critical review. Usually they have been approved by the President, and funds have been appropriated by Congress on the vague general assumption that such action is necessary to enable the armed forces to do their jobs. This attitude seems to take for granted that the United States has a solemn obligation to police the world and that the only function of Congress is to provide the essential funds.

In 1960, for example, the Eisenhower administration entered into an agreement with Ethiopia under which that country has been given more than $150 million in military assistance in return for the right to maintain a major American communications base, Kagnew Station, in Asmara. Congress knew vaguely that Kagnew was a hush-hush relay station for the Army's strategic communications system, a major naval communications center, a terminal for U.S. satellite systems, and an intelligence station for monitoring communications, particularly within the Soviet Union. About 3200 Americans in uniform and their dependents were stationed there. It was not until 1970, however, that Congress learned that the United States had also formally "reaffirmed" an interest in the security of Ethiopia and pledged its "opposition to any activities threatening the territorial integrity of Ethiopia." [5] That foggy and uncertain "commitment" was brought to light by the Symington subcommittee of the Senate in its investigation of American entanglements abroad.

David D. Newsom, Assistant Secretary of State for African Affairs, insisted that the agreement involved no commitment to defend Ethiopia, but it must have meant something to

---

[5] "Security Agreements and Commitments Abroad," report of the Senate Subcommittee on Security Agreements and Commitments Abroad, December 21, 1970, 91st Cong., 2d sess. (Washington: Government Printing Office), p. 9.

Emperor Haile Selassie or he would not have bargained for such a pledge. The net result of the agreement, moreover, was greatly to strengthen the Emperor's army, to provide him with American military advisers, a fleet of supersonic jet fighters, and bombs and ammunition that were used against insurgents in Eritrea. In other words, the United States became rather deeply involved with a tyrannical government for the sake of maintaining a secret electronic intelligence operation closely related to its self-assumed world-policing role.

Sharp questions ought to be asked as to whether the advantages from this kind of surreptitious activity offset its demoralizing effects on a great democratic power. If such facilities are imperative to our security, which is dubious, the least that can be demanded is that the arrangements be made in the open, through a treaty that can be examined by the Senate for any possible hidden commitments or excessive largess. The people have a right to know whenever their government indulges in a deal that could lead to embarrassing complications or the shedding of American blood. It is time to scrutinize every commitment that the military has dragged us into in the process of extending its hold upon strategic portions of the globe.

The proliferation of bases is not likely to be brought under control until Congress reasserts its authority in this area. The Symington subcommittee has pinpointed the obvious:

> Finally, and perhaps most important, the Congress should take a realistic look at the authority of the President to station troops abroad and establish bases in foreign countries. Notwithstanding the general authority which is contained in treaties and in Congressionally authorized programs, no U.S. forces should be stationed abroad or bases established abroad without specific prior authority of the Congress in each case.[6]

6 Ibid., p. 28.

Third. As we withdraw from the role of the lone policeman and give up the bases intended to support that role, it
becomes the more important to keep in good repair the
alliances that are really essential to our security. The most
vital of these is NATO. Whatever its shortcomings may be,
NATO is largely responsible for the peace that has prevailed
in Europe since World War II. Without it, Western Europe
probably could not have stemmed the Communist tide that
rolled over the satellite countries. With it, this cradle of
civilization has emerged from an era of destruction and near
despair into a period of economic progress and increasing
international cooperation. By comparison with other institutions growing out of this era of nuclear power and ideological
polarization, NATO is a resounding success. There is elementary wisdom in continuing to rely on it as the foremost
bulwark of our collective defense system.

NATO seemed to take a new lease on life at the meeting
of the foreign ministers of the fifteen member states at Brussels in December, 1970. The ten European members announced a build-up involving the investment of nearly $1
billion in organization, weapons, and armed forces during
the next five years. The offer to strengthen the European
contingents was designed to forestall any reduction in the
American troop level in NATO, then at 285,000 men. President Nixon responded in a statement read at Brussels by
Secretary of State Rogers. "Given a similar approach by our
allies," he said, "the United States will maintain and improve
its own forces in Europe and will not reduce them unless
there is reciprocal action from our adversaries." [7] If the
European members carry out their announced plans, this will
put the Soviet Union under pressure to agree to a joint
reduction of forces. And if no agreement is possible, a
revitalized NATO will be imperative to the security of the
free world.

[7] John M. Goshko in the *Washington Post*, December 4, 1970, p. 1.

Unfortunately, the NATO experience is not a reliable guide beyond the confines of the Atlantic community. No two regional security problems are sufficiently alike to justify attempts to transplant defense arrangements from one to another. Nevertheless, some ideas that have proved useful in one region may be advantageously adapted to another locale. The Organization of American States, for example, is urgently in need of some of NATO's cohesiveness. Probably the OAS will never organize standing defensive forces, as NATO has done, because they would tend to be dominated by the United States and our neighbors to the south would not trust us to be guided in all instances by a truly hemispheric policy. But the OAS could develop far more effective machinery than it now has for the organization of ad hoc peace forces when necessary. It could also move more expeditiously to protect basic hemispheric interests, instead of allowing its own inactivity to invite unilateral U.S. intervention. An overhauling of the OAS should have a high priority, but unfortunately our intervention in the Dominican Republic lays a critical handicap on any United States initiative in this matter.

When the United States gets its feet out of the mud in Vietnam, moreover, some kind of new deal in the Western Pacific will be in order. Relinquishment of the world policeman role should not involve abandonment of our interests in the Pacific, but we shall need something better than the Southeast Asia Treaty (SEATO) to guide the new era. SEATO is bankrupt if only for the reason that it was grossly abused by President Johnson as at least partial justification for his presidential war on the continent of Asia. This experience demonstrated that SEATO has a fatal flaw. In form and spirit it is a collective defense treaty, but it leaves each signatory free to act alone in case of an aggressive attack in the SEATO area. This makes a mockery of collective defense and gives a legal cover for any military venture that can be defended by one country as a response to aggression. It is not yet clear what should be put in the place of SEATO. Japan ought to be a major participant in any future collective peace-keeping system in the Far East, and Tokyo is not yet ready to determine what her role ought to be. Herman Kahn has suggested that because of their "pervasive and worldwide interests and capabilities" the Japanese may wish to take part in a peace-keeping role and that, "depending on events, this may be a surprisingly large part." [8] If Japan is willing, in the decades ahead, to continue relying upon the American nuclear umbrella and to put her great economic strength and possibly her conventional military prowess behind a policy for the Pacific region worked out jointly by the powers interested in that area, she can make an enormous contribution to peace and stability, both of which are essential to her emergence as a superpower. With Washington and Tokyo participating in such a security arrangement, they might well complement each other. The American presence would be a guarantee against any future Japanese imperialism in Asia. And Japan could doubtless be relied upon to guard against any future American venture of the Vietnam type.

In any event, the new security system, if one can be devised, should rest firmly on the basis of collective defense. Any decision to use external armed forces in the face of aggression, or a threat of aggression, should be taken only by joint action, after adequate consultation. Perhaps something less than unanimous agreement should be required, but at least majority action would be desirable. Some will object that a requirement for even majority action would handicap the peace forces in controversial cases, but that is the chief reason for requiring joint rather than individual operations. If the United States had consulted its SEATO

[8] Herman Kahn, *The Emerging Japanese Superstate* (Englewood Cliffs: Prentice-Hall, 1970), p. 8.

allies and waited for joint action before venturing into Vietnam with massive forces, the French and British would probably have saved us from a costly blunder. Indeed, French President Charles de Gaulle recorded in his *Memoirs* that he did warn President Kennedy, in regard to Indochina, that "you will, step by step, become sucked into a bottomless military and political quagmire despite the losses and expenditure that you may squander." [9]

The basic principle is that action taken in the name of collective defense should be in fact collective defense. One power's judgment is likely to be biased, faulty, or uninformed, and when doubt exists as to the necessity or the feasibility of armed intervention in any situation it is better to resolve the doubt against military operations rather than in favor of them. If the aggression is not such that it justifies war in the eyes of the majority, the sword should not be drawn. In some instances such a rule might leave wrongs unrighted, but we already have appalling evidence that an impulsive plunging in by one member of a collective alliance, acting alone, is a disastrous means of implementing an international policy.

A fourth essential element, if the retreat from globalism is to attain its ultimate objective, is an arms limitation agreement. As this is written the gloom resulting from the unproductive American-Soviet strategic arms limitation talks (SALT) is thick and pervasive. As early as July, 1970, the United States had put forward its proposal for a treaty, the core of which was a numerical ceiling on all offensive strategic weapons systems, including the Soviet's giant SS–9 missiles, and limitation or abolition of antimissile systems. But the Helsinki talks ended without any specific Soviet proposal, excepting a belated effort to limit the negotiations to antimissile (ABM) systems, with protection allowed for only Moscow and Washington. This was not acceptable to

[9] Henry Giniger in the *New York Times*, October 8, 1970.

the Nixon administration. Meanwhile the spirit of détente that had seemed to mark the opening of the negotiations had deteriorated into a new wave of suspicion and irritations. Some hope remained for ultimate agreement because of the obvious mutuality of interest in at least slowing down the perilous and futile race, which neither power can afford, but any potential breakthrough seemed a long way off.

The stubborn refusal of the USSR to make any concession or even to allow the ice of the cold war to melt gives an easy explanation of every failure in this sphere. But we should at least be aware of the fact that the whole equation has a very different look in Moscow. The Russians see the U.S.A. as the leader of the arms race from the beginning of the nuclear era. Since they have recently made gains vis-à-vis American nuclear strength, it is natural for them to hesitate about any agreement that might seem to narrow those gains. Given the much greater overall industrial capacity of the United States and our global network of military bases, moreover, the Russian inferiority complex is not without justification. In circumstances like these most of the gestures toward mutual understanding have to come from the power that is out in front.

Some military men and commentators see great danger in the recent Soviet build-up, especially in the continued deployment of the powerful long-range SS–9 missile. In December, 1970, Pentagon sources reported that the USSR had 350 SS–9s and was building them at a rate of 54 a year. Secretary of Defense Laird was quoted as saying that if this force of SS–9s should reach 420 "the Soviets will be able to wipe out 95 per cent of the U.S. force of 1,000 Minuteman missiles." [10] Similarly Laird feared that the Soviets' fleet of Yankee-class submarines may surpass the U.S. fleet of 41 Polaris submarines by 1974. The Soviet build-up appears to be real enough, and it has to be watched as one important

[10] *Newsweek,* December 14, 1970, p. 37.

element in the balance of terror that still exists between the two superpowers. But the Pentagon blows hot and then tepid about the SS–9 menace and is inclined to say less about American plans to equip half of its Minuteman missiles with multiple warheads and 31 Polaris submarines with new Poseidon missiles armed with up to ten warheads each.

These fears of what the Russians are doing are reminiscent of the scare campaign that was waged in the early 1960s over an alleged "missile gap" that was entirely imaginary. That propaganda led to a spurt in our nuclear armament program that in turn stimulated Moscow to greater efforts. Is the same process again in operation? How much of the talk of Soviet supremacy in potential missile warfare is designed to spur Congress into support of the Nixon administration's antiballistic missile program? If there is to be any hope for the limitation of strategic arms, Americans no less than Russians will have to keep their cool.

Some experts insist that the United States is still substantially ahead of the Russians in nuclear strength. But suppose the Soviet Union should attain some degree of superiority in the missile-counting game. So what? The bedrock fact is that each side has power to destroy the other but would itself be destroyed in the process. That fact has not changed, and it is not likely to change in the foreseeable future. A small margin of overkill on either side is far less important than an agreement to stop the endless proliferation.

Another element in the arms limitation dilemma was brought into sharp focus by the Symington subcommittee's final report. Despite the deep secrecy of the executive branch as to the location of nuclear weapons in foreign countries, the subcommittee noted that "United States tactical nuclear warheads have been and are stationed in countries all around the world, a pattern of deployment which results in arousing deep concern in both the Soviet Union and Communist China." [11] The extent of this scattering of nuclear weapons abroad is unknown to Congress and the public, although repercussions from the policy are frequently heard in the form of protests from the countries in which some of the weapons are supposed to be located. The State Department claimed that the subject was so strictly classified that it could not be discussed with the subcommittee investigating security agreements and commitments abroad under any circumstances. Some pertinent information was given to the Senate Foreign Relations Committee, but the general ignorance about this matter of vital concern in our international relations remains cause for alarm in a democratic country.

The Symington subcommittee summed up the incongruities and potential dangers of this provocative policy in the following paragraph:

> Should the Soviet Union or Communist China seek parity in the placement of tactical nuclear weapons to the point where one of them even approached the worldwide posture which the United States has today, we could face an international crisis comparable to that of the Cuban missile crisis of 1962. The United States went to the brink of nuclear war when faced with the possibility that the Soviet Union was putting missiles in a country ninety miles from the United States. We must assume that the Soviets, as they view our placement of tactical nuclear weapons in countries far closer to their borders than Cuba is to ours, will seek to break out of the nuclear ring that has been drawn around them.[12]

It is possible, of course, that our relations with the major centers of Communist power can never be trustful and

[11] "Security Agreements and Commitments Abroad," report of December 21, 1970, p. 13.
[12] Ibid.

friendly, but that remains to be seen. The Soviet Union and even China are undergoing evolution of their own, and events in the west are likely to have some influence on the directions they take. If NATO in the Atlantic community and a collective system in the Pacific could maintain low-profile defensive postures while providing economic and technical aid to promising underdeveloped countries, the odds in favor of free-choice societies could dramatically change in the years ahead.

In any event we need to acknowledge that we made colossal investments in military preparations and military ventures in the 1950s and the 1960s without really attaining the goals we were seeking. The time has come to try a different tack. Robert S. McNamara, who was once a leader in the overextension of our militarism, aptly posed the present challenge when he spoke as head of the World Bank in Copenhagen in September, 1970. "That twenty times more should be spent on military power than on constructive progress," he said, "appears to me to be the mark of an ultimate, and I sometimes fear, incurable folly." [13] What might have been accomplished if the hundred billion dollars that was squandered in Vietnam could have been devoted to nonmilitary enterprise designed to improve living conditions and enhance good will among peoples!

Progress in this direction would certainly entail abandonment of the last vestiges of cold war rhetoric. It would entail also patient, persistent, and long-range continuation of the efforts to attain a limitation of armaments. If such efforts fail this year, we should try again next year and in all the years following whenever there is even a glimmer of hope for success. Meanwhile the great and powerful United States of America can afford to forgo any competition in propaganda and rigorously eschew any attempt at trickery,

[13] *Washington Post,* November 30, 1970, p. A18.

double-dealing, or bomb rattling. Without letting down its guard and exposing itself to attack, it could shift its primary emphasis from military posturing and meddling all over the globe to a policy of prudent partnership and good neighborliness.

Fifth. A change in the international climate might be hastened by a sincere and energetic campaign to defuse the trouble spots that are now a source of much friction, fear, and potential disaster. The United States made an encouraging start in this sphere with the Rogers plan urging the hostile factions in the Middle East to "stop shooting and start talking." Under prodding from the State Department, Israel agreed to join in indirect negotiations through Gunnar V. Jarring, Special Representative of the United Nations. Egypt and Jordan accepted the plan, thereby recognizing Israel's right to exist. The negotiations came to an end when Israel accused Egypt of violating the military standstill along the Suez Canal, with the complicity of the Soviet Union. While adhering to its policy of maintaining the military balance in the Middle East, through additional aid to Israel, Washington worked for months to get the Jarring talks started again and finally succeeded. If this initiative should lead to only a precarious peace in the Middle East, the whole world could breathe easier. Baffling though the problem is, with Moscow supporting the Arab cause and Washington determined not to let Israel go down the drain, a measured drive for negotiations in a framework tolerable to both sides seems to hold the greatest hope of defusing the Middle East tinderbox.

Other trouble spots which invite a high order of statesmanship divorced from military posturing are Berlin and Taiwan. Berlin is primarily a problem for the Big Four powers that were victorious in World War II and the divided segments of Germany, while Taiwan is the foremost bone of contention

between the United States and China. Almost everyone
interested in calming troubled waters seems to agree that
something must give in regard to Taiwan. It is a patent
absurdity for the United States to continue pretending that
Chiang Kai-shek's regime on Taiwan is the legitimate government of mainland China. Of course we have a sixteen-year-
old mutual defense treaty with Taiwan, and since the island
can be readily defended by sea power, there is a strong argument for assisting in its defense against possible attack from
Communist China. But this is a very different matter. Adherence to the fiction that the Nationalist regime on Taiwan
might someday reestablish itself on the mainland is an unnecessary irritant and a drag on American prestige around
the world.

Even before the strange table-tennis diplomacy of 1971, the
Nixon administration sought some deflation of the
cold war with Communist China, mildly encouraging more
trade, travel, and communications, while continuing to op-
pose a seat for Peking in the United Nations. The emphasis
in the 1970 contest of the UN was on retaining a place for
Taiwan rather than denying a seat to Red China, although
the Nationalists insist that they will have no truck with the
UN if they are denied the big-power seat on the Security
Council that they have so incongruously held for a quarter of
a century. Despite the dogged opposition of both Peking and
Taipei, the United States thus seems to be moving toward a
two-China policy — the only outcome that is compatible with
current realities in the Far East.

Several observers have suggested a plebiscite on Taiwan
under international auspices. There are strong indications
that the Taiwanese would vote for independence from mainland China. Since it was the United States that took the
island from Japan in World War II, Washington could then
quite properly recognize the Taiwanese state and continue

the existing defensive alliance as a bulwark of peace in the Western Pacific.

Meanwhile, however, unnecessary provocations tend to keep animosities alive. In November, 1969, the United States was reported to have resumed reconnaissance flights over Communist China. Several joint U.S.–Taiwanese military exercises at least created an impression of cooperative plans to fight Red China. In pursuit of the same objective the Nationalist government tried to involve the United States more deeply in Taiwanese affairs. It extended the runways of two airfields, presumably in the hope that some of our military facilities on Okinawa, including nuclear-armed B–52s, would be transferred to Taiwan. Apparently the action was taken without any encouragement from Washington, and no plan to shift any bombers from Okinawa to Taiwan could be uncovered. The project was nonetheless provocative to Peking and undercut Washington's feeble efforts toward rapprochement. Here is a potentially explosive situation that calls for much more energetic and skillful defusing.

Finally, there is critical need for an understanding between the President and Congress on the use of the war power. Vietnam proved that Congress and the country no longer trust the President to order American troops into battle anywhere on the globe at his own discretion. But how can this reckless abuse of power be restrained without crippling the executive branch in the pursuit of security and other legitimate national interests? In several years of groping no ready answer has been found, but the rising opposition to undercover military operations abroad and to presidential grandstanding suggests that some solution will have to be found to avert the risk of chaos on one hand and complete loss of popular control over war-making on the other.

The refusal of the Supreme Court to hear Massachusetts' complaint (the Shea bill) that her sons were being drafted to

serve in an unconstitutional war — Vietnam — should be sufficient warning to Congress that the courts are not likely to
provide the answer. Courts are peculiarly unqualified to intervene in military matters. But Congress, with almost the
whole spectrum of power in this sphere assigned to it by the
Constitution, has ample means of making its will prevail. It
is a question of courage to assert itself or to seek a rational accommodation with the President that would enable both to
know where they stand.

Congress has made several efforts to reassert its war power
since the Vietnam venture went sour. After long prodding
from Chairman Fulbright of the Foreign Relations Committee, the Senate passed a resolution expressing its view that
armed forces or resources may be committed to the assistance
of another country only by "affirmative action taken by the
executive and legislative branches of the United States by
means of a treaty, statute, or concurrent resolution of both
houses of Congress specifically providing for such commitment." In December, 1969, Congress denied funds for any
American combat troops in Laos and Thailand. On two occasions the Senate voted to repeal the Tonkin Gulf resolution
of 1964, which had seemed to give the President a free hand
in Vietnam, and the House finally acquiesced. Then in the
turbulent last days of the 1970 session Congress wrote restrictions against the use of American forces in Southeast Asia
into three separate bills that became law.

Senators John Sherman Cooper and Frank Church were
the spearheads of this latter drive for reassertion of the congressional war power. Their amendments had the effect of
forbidding the use of any appropriated funds for the introduction of American ground combat troops or advisers into
Cambodia. The similar prohibition applicable to Laos and
Thailand was also continued. A third restriction was laid
upon the use of U.S. funds to pay foreign troops — South

Vietnamese, Laotian, or Thai — who might be engaged in combat in Cambodia and Laos. The President was authorized to lay aside this particular restriction if he should deem it necessary "to insure the safe and orderly withdrawal or disengagement of the United States Forces from Southeast Asia, or to aid in the release of Americans held as prisoners of war," [14] But this diluting language was not applied to the more important denial of funds for American ground troops and advisers. Congress also wrote into the law a proviso that the military and economic assistance approved for Cambodia should not be construed as a commitment to the defense of that country.

Sponsors of these restraints did not claim to have fashioned a straitjacket for the President. In the words of Senator Church, they acknowledged that the President has authority as commander in chief of the armed forces "to initiate action designed to protect American troops in the field . . . within a limited area." [15] But the debate made clear that the intent of the Senate, finally accepted by the House, was to forbid (unless specifically approved by Congress) any future expedition of American forces into Cambodia comparable to the 1970 raids on the sanctuaries. The President could, of course, ignore this mandate but only at the risk of setting Congress and the country against him, with the impeachment weapon lurking in the background.

Senator Church hailed the enactment of this amendment as "a historic moment. To my knowledge," he added, "this is the first time in the history of the United States that Congress has undertaken to write limitations into the law applying to the deployment of American troops abroad in the course of an ongoing war." [16] The achievement seemed to ac-

[14] *Congressional Record,* December 29, 1970, 91st Cong., 2nd sess., p. H12496.
[15] Ibid., p. S21396.
[16] Ibid., p. S21397.

quire additional significance because the restrictions were accepted by President Nixon and Secretary Rogers without a bruising fight over constitutional powers. Limited though the action was, it reestablished the right of Congress to constrain executive war-making by use of the spending power and put Congress on record for limiting the war in Southeast Asia.

These reforms did not inhibit the use of American air power in Southeast Asia or the continued use of special forces out of uniform in Laos. Geographically, too, their application was narrow. They must be regarded as only a beginning and not an end, yet they may prove to be an important step in the struggle against presidential wars. Certainly the White House is now on notice that it can no longer venture into military embroilments without risking congressional restraints and possibly a veto on spending.

There has been less concern in the House than in the Senate about presidential wars, but in November, 1970, the House did admonish the President to consult with Congress, "whenever feasible," before committing American troops to armed conflict. It also laid down some important reporting requirements. The House recognized, as of course it must, that the President has authority "to defend the United States and its citizens without specific prior authorization by the Congress," but only in "certain extraordinary and emergency circumstances." Representative Roman C. Pucinski pointed out that, by using the words "whenever feasible," the House was giving the President a handy bypass around Congress. In an effort to buttress the text by legislative history, however, he asserted that the President could use the bypass only "under the most extraordinary circumstances. Should he use the bypass frivolously," Pucinski added, "he does subject himself to severe censure and maybe even to impeachment." [17]

[17] *Congressional Record,* November 16, 1970, 91st Cong., 2nd sess., p. H10311.

Probably the most important aspect of the resolution was the requirement that the President promptly report to Congress if he should, without specific authorization, send military forces into battle, station them abroad, or substantially increase American forces already located in a foreign country. The President's report would have to set forth the circumstances necessitating the action, the constitutional or other authority under which he acted, the reason for not going first to Congress, the estimated scope of the operation, and other pertinent information. Hidden wars would thus become illegal. Congress would be confronted by at least some facts about any presidential military venture soon after its inception and could act accordingly.

Unfortunately, the Senate ignored this gesture from the House. In the 92nd Congress, however, a more hopeful start was made. The Senate Foreign Relations Committee promptly launched into hearings on several promising bills. Foremost among them was a bill by Senator Jacob K. Javits of New York specifically limiting the right of the President to initiate and carry on war without congressional sanction. The Javits bill would confirm the right of the President to use military force without a declaration of war (1) to repel a sudden attack on United States territory, (2) to repel an attack on U.S. armed forces legally stationed abroad, (3) to protect American lives and property, (4) to carry out a national defense commitment established by treaty or otherwise approved by Congress. But these emergency powers could not be stretched to cover a general war as they have been in the past. If Congress did not act within thirty days to sustain the President in such use of force, his authority to continue the action he had initiated would be ended. In effect, this would doubtless mean that, in all except the gravest emergencies, the President would go to Congress for authority before starting a military operation. The ingredients of a law restoring to Congress the prerogative of committing the country to war are readily at hand, and a mounting will to act is apparent. Transformation of the constructive ideas that have been advanced into practical legislation is probably the most important step that can be taken to bring our runaway militarism under control.

Somehow we must return to the principle so much cherished by the founding fathers: that one-man decisions committing the country to war are intolerable. In recent decades we have come to tolerate presidential wars on the assumption that they are essential to national defense, but the experience in the Bay of Pigs, Laos, and Vietnam suggests that they are more likely to lead us to disaster. The perils inherent in modern war make it imperative to revert to democratic checks on the President's impetuous coups. The disillusioned youth of America who are rebelling against presidential wars are following one of the oldest American traditions. In this matter, they are one in spirit with Jefferson, Madison, and most of the other founding fathers. It is time to recognize the legitimacy of this protest and to erect safeguards against military adventures that cannot withstand legislative scrutiny.

Restoration of the war power to Congress would probably have the effect of curtailing excessive militarism for the simple reason that 535 policy-makers are likely to move less readily into violence than one. Blind though it has often been to the dangers of militarism, Congress is now in a questioning mood. Many of its members are aware of the fact that militarism is blighting the hope of mankind at a time when science and technology have opened new vistas of amazing scope. Many are worried by the fact that the nations are spending some two hundred billion dollars annually on instruments and agencies of destruction and related activities at a time when disease, poverty, and ignorance are still rampant. It is a ghastly toll, and many conscientious legislators are troubled by the fact that the United States has been in the forefront of these military excesses. They see that our overbearing efforts to police the world have not only wasted enormous resources but also quickened the race that could end in the destruction of humanity.

Retreat from this passion to excel in every phase of the destructive art is, of course, a problem for the entire nation. It is not enough to say that our usurpation of the policeman's role reflects the instinct for self-preservation. Militarism begets militarism as certainly as hate begets hate. If we are not willing to risk anything for a live-and-let-live atmosphere, the result will be to risk everything by continuing to move toward a cataclysmic showdown. America should stand for something more around the globe than nuclear supremacy, military bases, and aid in the purchase of arms.

There is, of course, an extensive American commitment to many civilian interests abroad. The $100 billion American investment in Europe, our enormous and growing international trade, and the presence of two million American travelers abroad every year are indicative of a global activism in peaceful pursuits. But when that is accompanied by an excessive American military presence it is impossible to dissociate such commerce and communication from the suspicion of imperialism. We cannot hope to have the world accept our domestic concept of the U.S. as a benevolent, peace-loving country so long as the eagle (or the hawk) seems to be screaming everywhere and the dove cannot get out of its cage.

Fortunately, there are many evidences that a turn has come. A rapidly increasing number of people are sick of trying to cure every ailment of mankind with another bloodbath. Yet the basic objective of keeping militarism in its place and under rational democratic controls is frequently rejected by even the architects of the "new look." And some who commend the Nixon policy as at least a turn in the direction of realism continue to lament that no American solution of distant problems has been found.

Progress is thus painfully slow. How many decades will it take us to see our current stance astride the globe in true perspective?

Index

Index

241

Executive (presidential) authority: and Laos, 57–58, 60–61; and Congress, 231–236

Fairford Air Base, Britain, 29
Far East, 24, 190–209; and principle of collective security, 46; Japan as world power in, 204–208
Fishhook area, Cambodia, 101
"Flexible response" strategy, 18
Foreign Affairs, 207
Foreign Intelligence Advisory Board, 106–107
Foreign Service Institute, 8
Formosa, *see* Taiwan
"Forward defense" strategy, 18–19
401st Tactical Fighter Wing, 129
463rd Tactical Airlift Wing, 116
Fox, Robin, 211–212
France, 8, 19, 32, 67; and NATO, 22, 29, 151–152, 154; and SEATO, 47, 49; colonies in Indochina, 55; and nuclear power, 161
Franco, Francisco, 27, 128, 131, 133, 134, 141, 143–144, 179
Fulbright, Senator J. William, 36; and Bay of Pigs, 38–39; and Dominican episode, 43–44; and Laos, 58–60, 72–73; and Thailand, 79–80, 92; and Cambodia, 104–105; and U.S.–Philippines relations, 112, 117, 119–120, 125; and U.S. relations with Spain, 130, 139–140; and Senate hearings on U.S. bases in Japan and on Okinawa, 197; and reassertion of Congress' war-making powers, 232. *See also* Senate Foreign Relations Committee

Gaeta, Italy, 22
Garcia, Carlos P., 112
Geneva Accords, 54, 56, 60, 68–70; and North Vietnamese incursions into Cambodia and Laos, 101
Germany, *see* East Germany; West Germany
Gibraltar, 15, 132
Gideon, Lt. Gen. Francis G., 115, 117, 119
Globalism, 1–2, 9, 12–14, 24, 69, 74–75; and Nixon, 94, 109; and Spanish-American relations, 144; alternatives to, 210–238; and reduction of overseas bases, 218–220; and NATO, 221; and U.S. interests in Pacific, 222–224; and arms limitation agreement, 224–227; campaign to defuse potential trouble spots, 229; and restoration of Congress' war-making authority, 231–236
"Good neighbor" policy, 42
Goose Air Base, Canada, 23
Great Britain, *see* Britain

Greece, 22, 146, 151, 154, 168, 177–179; and Cyprus crisis (1964), 171, 174; and NATO, 178–179, 181, 182, 186, 188; and Communism, 179, 180; U.S. aid to, 179, 183; military junta, 180–188; political apathy, 183–185; U.S. reticence about interfering in affairs of, 185–186; and Council of Europe, 186–187
Green, Senator Theodore F., 48
Greenland, 23
Greenock, Scotland, 21
Grey, Gordon, 107
Grossetto Air Base, Italy, 30
Guam, 26
Guantánamo Bay, Cuba, 23
Guatemala, 38

Haile Selassie, Emperor of Ethiopia, 220
Hannah, John A., 73
Hare, Ambassador Raymond A., 172
Healey, Denis, 155
Helms, Richard, 71
Ho Chi Minh Trail, 57, 65, 69
Holy Loch, Scotland, 21
Hong Kong, 15
House of Representatives, U.S., 234; Foreign Affairs Committee, 17. *See also* Congress
Hudson Institute, 206
Hughes, Charles Evans, 177
Huks, 119, 122
Hungary, 148

ICBM (intercontinental ballistic missile), 5, 6; in three-pronged nuclear defense system, 7
Iceland, 151
Imperialism, 3, 24
Incirlick Air Base, Turkey, 174
India, 8, 15, 208
Indochina, 49, 55, 100, 216
Inönü, Ismet, 171, 172
Institute for Strategic Studies, 5
Inter-American Treaty of Reciprocal Assistance (1947), 36, 45; Organ of Consultation, 36–37
International voluntary service, 66
Iraklion Air Station, 22
Iraq, 15
Isolationism, 215
Israel, 20, 229
Italy, 21, 22, 29, 186; and NATO, 151, 154
Itazuki Air Base, Japan, 194, 198
Iwakuni Naval Station, Japan, 198

Japan, 2, 8, 67, 190–209; U.S. military bases in, 16, 24–25, 30, 193, 195–200; U.S. relations with, 190–209; postwar political periods, 190–191; and U.S. bases on Okinawa, 190–192, 200–202, 205, 208; economic recovery,